The PERSISTENCE *of* LIBERTY

The
PERSISTENCE
of
LIBERTY

An American Philosophy

DAVID ROSS NETHERTON

Hermes Editions
Boston

A HERMES BOOK
Published by Hermes Editions
A Division of Hermes Boston
31 Milk Street
PO Box 960029
Boston, Massachusetts 02196

This book is an original publication of Hermes Editions

The Persistence of Liberty: An American Philosophy
Copyright © 2019 by David Ross Netherton

Cover design Masayo Ozawa

Book design by Colin Rolfe

All rights reserved. This book, or parts thereof, may not be reproduced in any form without written permission.

PRINTING HISTORY
Hermes hardcover edition / November 2019

Library of Congress Control Number 2019909059

ISBN Hardcover 978-1-948796-78-1
ISBN Paperback / Softcover 978-1-948796-79-8
ISBN eBook 978-1-948796-80-4

Text from "Final Oral Exam," *Harvard Magazine* (1980) noted in Chapter Nine used by permission.

With God on Our Side by Bob Dylan Copyright © 1963 by Warner Pros. Inc.; renewed 1991 by Special Rider Music. All rights reserved,International copyright secured. Reprinted by permission; *My Back Pages* by Bob Dylan Copyright © 1964 by Warner Bros. Inc.; renewed 1992 by Special Rider Music. All rights reserved. International copyright secured. Reprinted by permission; *Shelter from the Storm* by Bob Dylan Copyright © 1974 by Ram's Horn Music; renewed 2002, by Ram's Horn Music. All rights reserved. International copyright secured. Reprinted by permission.

Publication and distribution
EPIGRAPH PUBLISHING
NEW YORK

10 9 8 7 6 5 4 3 2

For Joanne

"If one advances confidently in the direction of his dreams, and endeavors to live the life he has imagined, he will meet with success unexpected in common hours."
— Henry David Thoreau, *Walden*

CONTENTS

Preface — xi

1 BOOK OF HABITS — 1
CHAPTER ONE Modus Vivendi — 3
CHAPTER TWO Popular Alienation — 11
CHAPTER THREE Inheriting Nostalgia — 18
CHAPTER FOUR Bebop Doo-wop — 26
CHAPTER FIVE Dreams of Disaster — 36

2 BOOK OF HERESIES — 45
CHAPTER SIX Letter to Abigail — 47
CHAPTER SEVEN Ordinary Alchemy — 56
CHAPTER EIGHT Double Souls — 65
CHAPTER NINE Waiting for Change — 72
CHAPTER TEN Hymn to Hypatia — 82

3 BOOK OF VOYAGES — 93
CHAPTER ELEVEN Kansas Valkyrie — 95
CHAPTER TWELVE Tempo di Valse — 102
CHAPTER THIRTEEN Café Vandal — 112
CHAPTER FOURTEEN Doctrine's Orders — 123
CHAPTER FIFTEEN Supreme Futures — 133

4 BOOK OF VISIONS — 139

CHAPTER SIXTEEN National Endowments — 141
CHAPTER SEVENTEEN Video Incest — 147
CHAPTER EIGHTEEN Twisted Fate — 156
CHAPTER NINETEEN Bert Lonestone, Left Field — 165
CHAPTER TWENTY Mei Kuo — 176

Chapter Epigraphs — 186
Index — 190

Preface

This book does not pretend to be an accurate social history. It has no greater ambition than to remind the reader that each generation lives with its irony. As a group of essays, it owes much to American essayists Franklin, Emerson, Poe, Bierce, Twain, and S.J. Perelman—among others—though perhaps a straighter line may be drawn from the engaging *Prejudices* of H.L. Mencken.

The essential quality and character of America emerged from a handful of simple principles. In such a broad view of thought and experience, one can reasonably expect to discover and rediscover irony. Unifying themes of liberty, music, architecture, and literature appear, along with revolutions in the natural sciences, evolution of the spirit, and in general, how to use space and time.

Unlike characteristic *lyrical philosophy* in the Chinese tradition of personal experience, this book is meant rather as *practical philosophy*. The broad discipline of practical philosophy requires insights into the nature of actions, persons, values, and reasons. It has to do with what Americans have in common.

In this edition, the *Book of Habits* recalls the spirit of America at mid-century, commitment to style and expanding the horizons of the possible, a progressive design for living, the American "suitcase of remembrances," and urban sophistication contrasted with suburban sensibility. The *Book of Heresies* recollects the problem of leisure, secret knowledge, racism and wars, self-reliance and over-education, and women and wisdom.

The *Book of Voyages* revisits young Americans abroad, empires, villages and myth, global human development, and preoccupations with the future. The *Book of Visions* relives architecture and culture, what one knows that can't be taught, universal vision and modern ethics, baseball at the speed of light—and finally, liberty and the joyful flow of undirected thought.

It is my pleasant duty to acknowledge that preparation of this book has been possible only with the help of others. The thread of an idea often is woven into the fabric of thought by many hands. For their encouragement and indulgence, I am grateful to Nan and Ross Netherton. The idea for this book originally was the notion of Ruth Roberta Hedrick Livingston, part of a conversation near Mrs. Bohannon's garden. I am indebted to Richard Bruce Netherton and Nancy Netherton Stelling for both their wit and realistic sensibility born of countless nightshifts. Mr. Ma and staff at the Harvard-Yenching Institute have instructed me in Mandarin texts and translations. I have been assisted in the preparation of the manuscript by Cheryl Gordon White, and I thank her for her skill and patience.

Insights and suggestions of Joanne Bruno Netherton, to whom this book is dedicated, have in every case improved it. For their many individual contributions, original observations, and humor, I am grateful to our sons Ross and Myles. For any errors that remain, I alone bear responsibility.

DRN
Boston & London, 2019

1

BOOK OF HABITS

Recalling decades of the fifties and sixties…

A design for living reaffirmed original ideas despite apparent losses of consciousness, growing self-indulgence, and plain blundering.

Society wandered back to school in large numbers, seeking formulae for modern life and material gratification.

The American sense of history stretches back only a few decades, kept in a suitcase full of remembrance.

The essence of hipness contemplated beatniks, suburban mentality, and self-commentary.

Fantastic utopias and the ecstasy of discovery receded under the anodizing construction of equanimity and the situation comedy.

CHAPTER ONE

Modus Vivendi

Life is something to do when you can't get to sleep.
— Fran Lebowitz

While Voltaire was struggling to understand the nature of human existence in a cosmos governed by rational principles, impersonal laws, and sublime ideas, rough and lonely Puritans were setting about a propitious enterprise. So began a nation of first principles—its own. The warp of the venture had a heady conviction of free and public use of critical reason, individualism rather than tradition, and an enduring democratic experiment. Early on, Voltaire had hit upon the philosophical conception of *liberty*—freedom from tyranny and restraint, encouraging debate, and the ethics of right action.

Emerging from a mixture of brilliant intellectual argument and violent rebellion in the eighteenth century, America began a progressive parade of demonstration projects. The wondrous part was that, in this place, optimism seemed to be the necessary and sufficient driving force. Rational men had taken the trouble to come and inspect the New World a hundred years after the Revolution, and had pronounced it big and energetic. The essence of this place that had seduced everyone who arrived in the past fifteen thousand years was *horizon*.

Now, anything is going to seem big when you are coming from a hopelessly overcrowded village east of the Tisza, piled on top of antiquity covered over by medieval cellars. But there had been others here too—the first nations—that is, people who had come when the animals did. So beckoning and vast was this horizon as to imbue the native race with a sort of peripatetic spiritualism, encouraging migration on foot between the Big Waters—prompted by those elemental forces: the winds, the equinoxes, the Maine black fly.

It is in the nature of humans, not just Americans, that our progress be according to sequential steps. In its essential character, human progress has gone something like this: coming in from the rain, a gift from Prometheus, body paint, Giza, rice, the sail, the alphabet, taxes.

Before life was conscious of itself, there was motion. Once conscious of motion, the preoccupation is with direction. The preferred direction is toward better and better. Gradually, it is evident that how we do things matters. Human motion needs to be upward and outward.

Sixty generations ago, a certain design for living emerged, now barely recognizable. Around the year 800 CE, things began to happen. Buildings of glorious extravagance were erected in Java, Malaysia, and throughout Indochina. The Pallavas lost their grip on southern India, and the great ragas were codified. Gregorian chant took hold in Europe. Alfred of Britain became the Great by virtue of his success in war followed by a set of legal tenets through which it was thenceforth to be avoided. Charlemagne was crowned Emperor. The first Vikings were born—those men and women whose issue would end up ruling Europe.

What made this extraordinary period different from previous millennia and made its thought and way of life so enduring was not so much that behavior changed. Rather, people began to examine life, laud it, glorify it, and actually define the best of it.

That this was done mostly through the arts is to many particularly encouraging. Ragnar of the Hairy-Breeks may have continued his forebears' habit of sacking Paris, but now his Icelandic scribes were committing it all to poetic sagas. Humans listened to poetry and the imperfect polyphony of Limoges and Rheims. They observed the law, respected the word and revered the illuminated manuscript. These artifacts showed how to live, even why. There was glory in living.

For most Americans, it is a natural feeling that things should be getting better—bent on progress and looking to improve. Since the Romans introduced capitalism, many have labored under Western notions of *civilization*—meaning participating, designing, and managing life. Still some have come to think of civilization as culture, and culture as pleasurable things that happen accidentally.

Yet what we call *culture* includes ideas, especially favorite ideas, that are real in some way or other. Culture is a reminder of which way is up. Art has a connection with culture many have struggled to describe. Societies cannot decide whether culture produces its art or is the result of it. Taste, of course, includes bad taste by which beauty is ignored or, more often, mistaking something banal for something beautiful.

It's been suggested that the need to gain a living certainly influences art. The artist may sometimes seek anonymity so that the art as beauty is free to take care of itself. All art in this sense is unfinished and imperfect, and awaits its completion through someone else's good taste. Leonardo complained to his patrons more than once about distractions of hunger and penury. He thought his work was lacking due to the absence of tranquility. Rarefied genius, one is reminded, must also be capable of turning a ducat.

All this suggests the need for a predicate for life. Given choice, something should show how to choose. This is culture's domain.

Culture may be considered an end, an ideal, or simply a point of view. As an end, culture is something consciously aimed for, something to be achieved through concerted effort and energy, movement from less to more refined. Rooted in self-cultivation, this sense of culture is conscious and deliberate; however, culture encourages movement beyond limitations and recalls pre-historical impressions. By contrast, culture as ideal is unconscious and subjective.

The American strategy from the beginning has been *abundance*. It rests on assumptions about the virtue of material wealth and the appetite for durable possessions. Abundance, though, as many off-shore observers of American culture will not hesitate to add, is lacking without a sense of possibility and necessary commitment to style.

Americans—critics go on—lose everything in the religion of accumulation, for plenty can just as easily be vice as virtue. Proficiency at one thing or other counts as nothing toward culture when the proficient are blind to other qualities they lack. This argument concludes that whatever the system produces, it is witness to numberless bedraggled youth who have not been taught what they need in order to survive. They are empty in the midst of abundance.

American culture, some fear, for all its energy and proficiencies may eclipse all higher human achievement and overrun something altogether better. One response to this has been the tentative proposition that democracy *is* culture. It may be true that in time, democracy will create a new array of values in art and literature. Practical democracy, though, has a leavening effect on the masses. Democratic society regards humanity and the neighborhood in exactly the same terms, giving reason to hope great artists can emerge as easily from fairness as from subjugation.

Language has been used as a measure of culture. Poetry, with its refinement and abstract quality, has been suggested as a universal index to a society's culture. Not surprisingly, it is mostly poets who suggest this—English poets in particular. The English language is rich in rhythms acquired from other cultural sources: Saxon verse; Norman-French poets; and Welsh, Scots, and (of course) the Irish writers. Some Irish have argued for English to be regarded as a common property rather than a distinct, exclusive, somehow superior tongue. The Gaelic galaxy certainly has upped the ante for the creative use of English.

If Italy and France claim painting and Germany claims music, England may be left with poetry as its cultural boast. The English especially emphasize the Romantic movement. English is now filled with Teutonic mutations from the Greek in Goethe, and Latin antecedents arriving through

Baudelaire and the French Impressionists. In this vein, America can stand to make more of its son of Irish extraction, Edgar Allen Poe, for the way he raised the poetic quotient.

No single culture sustains for long its lofty creativity in poetry, and this makes it interesting as one marker for the rise and fall, ebb and flow of the sublime. Spanish, Arabic, Persian, Japanese, and Indian poetry—each has its classical age. Poetry offers a posy for the perplexed, serving the same function in any culture. It puts life in language and, through its more ethereal parts, raises culture to what Keats called the "cerebral apartments," there to relive better moments.

Provocative research in the last century, conducted by a small group believing there may be a cultural component to the neurobiology of learning and remembering, concluded that listening to piano sonatas enhances spatial and temporal reasoning. Investigators report that exposure to music, like mathematics and chess, changes thinking by changing the physical architecture of the brain. It encourages movement toward survival and improvement, and generally feeling better. They insist music plays a special role in higher cognitive functions. Mozart seems to show the greatest effect.

Things break down a bit though, in trying to explain the "Mozart Effect." Apparently, it is described by a certain pattern in which neurons fire. A map of the common neural structure of the cortex can be rendered, its symmetry computed, and a convincing analysis distilled. Evidently, Mozart's spatiotemporal firing patterns were well-established by age four, when he composed the early sonatas.

Experimental subjects get progressively better (more Mozart-like) as they latch onto the master's music. They approach genius ever so slowly, or perhaps just metaphorically. Still, it's not clear what really happens while "learning." What is happening to the cultural self? Does the subject merely emulate genius—gravitate to what feels potent? Can one ever do anything more? Who, the world wondered, can ever fire neurons with Amadeus? Then Beethoven sits down at the keyboard. Culture is suddenly anti-aristocratic, less hygienic, and not quite so well-behaved. Yet it has moved higher; it is more universal. It cannot stop itself.

There is ample evidence that any major city both illustrates culture and shows the effects of its death. Central metropolitan districts often are the unwilling repositories of cultural refugees—escapees from conventional life, the nameless, the hapless, the feckless. Lotus eaters and stargazers endure only for a short span. Their frame of reference is so large as to be useless for survival. Constant winter lives in their purple souls. No one cares how their neurons are firing. Theirs is a homeless wish for early retirement from humanity in the general direction of oblivion.

Innate and introspective, culture is an echo to set our bearings. Architect, practical philosopher, and futurist Buckminster Fuller suggested that having to earn a living through some drudgery as justification for existence is a specious notion and should be abandoned. He declared that people instead should, "think about whatever it was they were thinking about before somebody came along and told them they had to earn a living." The instinct to celebrate one's own personal situation can actually become habit.

There is a paradox in the notion of American "Eurocentrism." The United States has lived under the same constitution for longer than its European cousins. In the same period, France has had five republics, fascism, a commune, and two empires. England produced the Magna Carta but never a constitution. Germany and Italy were squabbling in their many regions and did not even become countries until the late-nineteenth century.

From Europe, America inherited concepts of the rule of law, one person-one vote, and representative government. To these, America added the precepts of freemasonry, namely self-reliance and the sovereignty of the individual, and from Puritan beginnings: enterprise, ingenuity—then imagination.

Ever since one George Downing had, in 1642, become the first graduate of the College in Newtowne, Massachusetts Bay (later Harvard, in Cambridge) with a degree in the science of business administration, Americans have been absorbed in education. Downing may have returned to become a London slumlord with a certain street of some local interest today bearing his name, but he had started something here.

At the halfway point of the century, Americans began to harp on the idea that there was great potential here. Horizons of the possible expanded in the midst of freedom to make choices. The American harp was tuned to the frequency of liberty.

CHAPTER TWO

Popular Alienation

Whither goest thou, America, in thy shiny car in the night?
— Jack Kerouac

Numbers change life. Americans had spurred Allied Forces to triumph in World War II and set about making many more Americans. The War had brought the industrial conversion of the United States, carried out with scarcely a break in stride. With the pressure of numbers—markets changed, political thought changed, expectations changed, and even the weather seemed to be improving.

Thinking changed, too. There was less of it. That is, with so many more around to do the thinking, there was no real increase in the number of new ideas. By contrast with recent decades this was peculiar. There quickly appeared a sort of emotional inflation that felt comfortable, and many just stopped looking for problems. Intellectuals who make it their business to uncover problems could do no better than to isolate, then describe, the "leisure problem." Affluence, it turned out, could come to just about everyone. A home in Levittown, New York was now available for fifty-eight dollars a month. The GI Bill enabled millions of new fathers to enrich themselves with a college degree, many receiving an education.

All things seemed to move in colossal waves of very little activity. Popular tendencies became black holes swallowing all deviations, and a lot of initiative. American institutions had won stunning victories, so why shouldn't everything be incorporated into routines? Fanning out from the languid dome of Washington, the habit of conforming sought to neutralize anxiety as it seeped into offices, bars, coffee houses, and the living room.

Eisenhower was president, and it was no good him trying to ignore it. Dwight D. Eisenhower was thought to be the best writer among all the Army's generals. As Supreme Commander of Allied Forces, Ike had moved a fair number of well-decorated figures around on Europe's chessboard, some of whom were quite theatrical in their enthusiasm. Ike seemed to maintain a rational contempt for war while going about the demanding business of being decisive. Good as he had been with military strategy and concrete maneuvers, his mind apparently wandered from time to time. It wandered so much, in fact, that Columbia University asked him to be their president.

Nothing functioned independent of the influence of Eisenhower's presidency. This was folklore with the self-indulgence the country demanded. Paranoia in a rather homogenized state took up most of the good hours of the day and America was pleased to support not so much a working, thinking president as a figurehead with full clusters. Government now was managerial. If denied Adlai Stevenson—well, there were Mike Nichols and Elaine

May. The country was, after all, about the consuming task of settling into a new and grander heritage. Attention spans were retracting.

Alienation became popular. American alienation took a curious form in that the practitioner was able to indulge to the extent of his or her belief and conviction.

What America was succumbing to was affluence in the absence of war. It made many scared, depressed, nervous, and constipated. There were more and more who were better off but surrounded by the rest of the world. An uncomfortable cynicism emerged that began to turn to romance, idealism, and religious fervor. High fidelity stereo sound helped. Cars took up an increasing proportion of time, budget, and daydreaming. A new purpose was conceived as the perfection of engineering the bejesus out of playthings. It was a way everyone could avoid the moral issues and get on with it.

The dominant social construction of reality, however, was the formula for rational procrastination. A lot of what came out of the early 1950s never actually escaped the decade. It occurred to Americans that there was a great deal of unfinished business and time lost to the war. Congress was publicly excused and any work requiring moral judgment was deferred. After national movements of economic recovery from the Depression in the thirties and the Allied war effort of the forties, the United States was undefeated in team competition. Time had been called by 1950, and the country developed a reactive outlook. The obvious job now was to redeem gratification coupons accumulated over the last twenty years. Thanks to the enormous potential of an organized and efficient industrial machine, the dividends could be distributed to every precinct. Time and money were universally applied to what would become characteristically American pursuits of happiness, recognized by their frivolous and whimsical properties. Again, the pressure of large numbers changed things.

Peace of the era, alas, brought with it no peace of mind. So it was that, in the boom economy, short-term memory was all anyone exercised. Rules of history did not obtain. Our badinage through the early years of the century—the United States emerging from the Great War as the industrial and financial power of the world—was legend. But this *age of prosperity* had the soft underbelly of isolationism.

Victory in World War II also had come through the stern efforts of the Commonwealth Nations; the stealth of the French underground; innumerable acts of individual courage in Scandinavia, Poland, and Czechoslovakia; and through the coordinated effort of a dozen Western nations. Victory had been all the more decisive through the final achievement of a cadre of foreign-born physicists working on the Manhattan Project. The American uniform had stood out in relief against the backdrop of European culture. Millions of Americans had had the opportunity to size up Europe firsthand then head home.

For the first half of the century, Americans had been unique in the way leaders are: individual, iconoclastic, and a little untidy. The uniqueness of America in the eyes of Europeans now was simply that it was somehow different. The new and unshakable impression was that, individually, Americans were wholly another species—apparently not fully evolved. This was something like visiting the home office with a stupendous annual report in hand and being treated with all the deference and detachment due a branch manager. The most damaging of the phantoms landing back in the United States from Europe was self-criticism, the psychic companion to isolation.

But prosperity, like guilt, is psychological, and two visionaries helped immensely here. Plumbing the finer points of human motivation, the odd pair of John Maynard Keynes and Walt Disney, working separately, had crafted the foundation for modern American life. Keynes had tirelessly described the capitalistic system and run sufficient theoretical dollars through the model for the concept to be truly seductive. Disney, on the other hand, was in the business of creating the American consumer culture, that is to say "entertainment." Each has an enduring influence on American society. There's still nothing like Walt Disney for scaring the shit out of little kids.

With cheap methods of reproduction firmly in place, the virulent new phenomenon, "mass culture," was at hand. Unlike folk art of the past, it was produced not spontaneously but commercially and continuously by paid directors, artists, writers, and composers—for huge audiences. It was concocted for consumers and had the great benefit of requiring no contemplative thought, judgment, or reflection. This was to be sheer spectacle—and movies, television, LPs, and comic books all qualified. At first, there were forebodings that mass culture would compete with, and even drive out, "high culture"—serious works of art, literature, good music. Nonsense. It was soon clear that entertainment couldn't care less about high culture, and why should it? The whole point was to avoid the deep issues and glide into spontaneous pleasures. Joy, irony, tragedy, wit, originality, and beauty in everyday life were basically unsalable, and those herculean artists of high culture who died crazy and destitute were expected to be dead a long time.

It can be a great efficiency to simply adopt ideas without troublesome inquiry. Insecurity that lingered in the air was countered with a defense of conformity. The voice of the majority was commonly received and the echo was deafening. In conformity there was strength, and public and private institutions—schools, churches, factories, little league—became socializing agencies bending to the pull of gravity. There was no fun in supporting the eccentric, and it might even be dangerous. Straying too far to the left or right jeopardized ever finding the way back again. The path was narrow if not always straight. Freedom of thought and intellectual energy were to be excused for a while.

Too many cooks mix their metaphors, so everyone headed in the same direction. Competition for status among neighbors suffused things of the age with mystical properties. If everyone did not achieve genuine status, there was a universal leap of faith that allowed symbols of status. Status symbols neatly fit the progressive formula for life. They were neither cherished and rare *objets d'art* from the past, nor comfortable old books. They were big, noisy, complicated, unnecessary, and hard to ignore—so everybody else knew about them. Most of all, they were expensive but accessible—and at their best, disposable, allowing for the periodic exploration of newer ones. Better yet, get two or three. "In a country where every man is only what he has," intoned the anonymous butler, "he who has nothing is nobody very much."

As a status symbol, the automobile was not only accessible, useful, expensive, and ultimately disposable; it was also handsomely equipped. Beyond the kitchen, there was no single space which could be loaded with as many attention-getting conveniences as the car. The legacy of the automobile rolled on. Besides creating the suburbs and its attendant art forms, the automobile in large numbers made it possible for the country resident to leave his and her isolation in the wilderness and get to know firsthand, and on a regular basis, the isolation of the city. There was still the freedom to choose one's isolation.

On October 4, 1957, Moscow moved America off its complacent center with the launching of the first space satellite: Sputnik I (Traveler). Sputnik II took up a dog a month later, and that did it. What a military expert called "the limited imagination and limited budget of our space program," were re-evaluated. American slackness and anti-intellectualism had gotten a real jolt. In the next year, the United States brought out the Explorer, Vanguard, Pioneer, and the Atlas series. These satellites were not on the planetary scale of the Russian series but were going farther with each outing. Society wandered back to school in large numbers.

CHAPTER THREE

Inheriting Nostalgia

*The older I get, the more vivid is my recollection
of things that never happened.*

— Mark Twain

Traveling light is not the American habit. Much of the world can get by with a bedroll; some need a valise and others insist on a weekend case. Americans take the Pullman and haul a steamer trunk if possible, to ensure that each trip is both memorable and comfortable. Content only when everything is at hand, each American prefers to carry a personal emporium of worn memorabilia.

Every act of packing up in preparation for leaving has already started on the return trip to the familiar. Readily setting out for new territory demands every weight of available psychic apparel. Yet of all the directions pondered, the best is simply to go back. Nostalgia is more the American habit. So where does this nostalgia actually take the traveler?

It frequently leads back no more than a generation. In the fifties, many seemed to regret having missed the Depression—as if it was a kind of national park. The Great Depression in the thirties, for example, now can appear to be a petrified forest of cultural nationalism. There were compelling stories with morals, sad tales of separation, fables of hardship. It sent families in the direction of old-time religion and new philosophy. The decade of the thirties oddly ginned-up America's characteristic yearning for the "sweet-used-to-be."

Nostalgia, as practiced in mid-century America, was a burlesque of legend and longing. The ironic commentator Lenny Bruce reminded everyone that "what should be never did exist, but people keep trying to live up to it." Yet there was plenty of theatre and style amid the thirties rubble when much of the nation was literally on the road. The traveling circus kept the business of dreams alive in thousands of remote towns across Kentucky, the Dakotas, Arizona, Oklahoma, and everywhere there were fifty people within a day's walk. The empty vessel of wonder was filled by mystics and sideshows.

More changes had been visible in the city. The heavy air of trial had brought many things to a halt. Divorce was one of them. If families were apart, it was often through the tragedy of men having finally reached a breaking point in anguish and humiliation—and mothers with children having to find a home for themselves somewhere else. Many families tended to stay together, even at great distances, their men drifting from place to place in search of work that someday would reunite them. But it's continually demonstrated that divorce is something Americans customarily rediscover just as quickly as they can afford it.

Other sorts of romantics had drifted from place to place in the thirties, but these fellows had long since abandoned hope of reunion with anything of permanence. They rode the rails, slept in barns, cooked over an open fire, and created their own art. The American hobo was distinguished from the bum and the vagrant in that he sometimes worked. Simultaneously urban wrangler and survivor in the wilderness, "hobohemians" traveled the great railway system as one continuous lived-through memory, riding from Texarkana up to Chicago, over to Akron—and on to Reading and Richmond—then Savannah, St. Louis, Abilene, Tucson, and Bakersfield. This memory of the hobo became a daydream of individual fulfillment. Self-reliance and pioneering persisted here in a brotherhood that gave dignity to the destitute.

War forestalls serious inquiry. This meant that our intellectual inheritance of the 1950s was mostly that vigorous and prolific literary period of the 1930s. By comparison with any other time in the century, there was compelling conversation going on in America during the thirties. The case for modern American prosperity was not the romantic idealism of the nineteenth century; so what, exactly, was the twentieth-century American mind so nostalgic about?

Part of it was a literary nostalgia that yearned for the many gifted and courageous writers active in the thirties, most of them voting communists. A dozen or so writers marked out America intimately, gripped by a new spirit they saw as half-heartedly searching out something fundamental. Sherwood Anderson and Waldo Frank were at the vanguard of this literary nostalgia. Most of these earlier figures wrote in intimate styles on customarily unmentionable themes with a candid and uncompromising fashion that broke the ice for the younger Hemingway, Wolfe, and Faulkner—and all who followed.

Perhaps it all began in 1930, after Sinclair Lewis had won the Nobel prize for literature. America, to him, was strange, complex, and inscrutable, so he wrote of the small town with a sardonic view. Lewis was unapologetic. His indictments were not angry satire but slaps at what he saw as the betrayal of the promise of the bourgeoisie. The importance of Sinclair Lewis in the fifties was simply that, by then, most of the world had read him.

Monumental expatriates Hemingway, Dos Passos, and Wolfe had studiously courted Ezra Pound and Gertrude Stein—and had come to a style that replaced abstraction and romanticism with what often seemed a rather uninviting monosyllabic cement. Hemingway accepted death and disaster as part of the fun of it all and looked to the strong and brave to put some order to the confusion of life and the elements of it he loved so well: war, violence, dissipation.

Writers are as nostalgic as anybody else. At a certain point in American literary indulgence, one seemingly had to have driven an ambulance in a foreign war to sit at the typewriter with any moral conviction. Dos Passos qualified, and it quickly got him away from nymphean dreams of America and into industrial politics. There was political infidelity on a grand scale.

Thomas Wolfe, by contrast, was an energetic, undisciplined, lyrical genius with longings derived from the country scene welling up in American rural family life. His *You Can't Go Home Again* remains the American standard in the category of nostalgia. Like Wolfe, William Faulkner conjured townspeople whose stories are a revealing social history. His renditions of the South—for many below the Mason-Dixon, America's only real crack at its own aristocracy—spread through Europe and beyond.

By mid-century, prose writing in America was thought to have run out its remarkable string. Older writers with reputations made in the thirties were no longer turning out books of substance. Readers and critics turned to familiar European writers who dealt with dismay and angst. Many simply turned to the past for nostalgic comfort. Some liked to climb the writers' staircase between the thirties and the fifties in the company of Steinbeck and O'Neill. Others took the freight elevator with Clifford Odets.

One book set down largely during the thirties that explained life thenceforth with humorous insight could be found on many a home bookshelf in the 1950s. It was *The Thurber Carnival*. James Thurber's infectious stories were coveted by anyone who could read. He nostalgically reconciled the Civil War with the Industrial Revolution, explained the political yahoo, the automobile, and your certifiable old grandfather up in the attic. Such popular nostalgia made possible the great sticking on of American opinions. Their origins may have been obscure, but these opinions were the fundamental precepts whose indelible presence had brought everyone to the middle of the twentieth century.

Writer's nostalgia was just one means of imparting the American consensual point of view. Consensus was in the streets, and of course, in the schools. There simply was nobody around to contest the arbitrary national bill of particulars.

First, *the pursuit of happiness* is an American constitutional guarantee and it's right up there with life and liberty as the major orders of business. Luckily, happiness was easily defined. Its pursuit was constant and unrelenting, a sort of high-speed chase.

Second, *competition made America great*, and the keepers of the flame were corporations, private colleges, organized sports, and chambers of commerce. There is room for honor and fairness in competition, but the whole idea is to pay enough attention to be victorious. Competitors are there to be vanquished—adversaries utterly defeated.

Third, *scouting builds character*. As everyone knows, doing your part is essential. Scouting had a leg up here. There was a reverence attached to the scout's baldric-and-badge regalia, signifying the sacrifice of otherwise happy days of play to outings in county wetlands. Although there were comparatively few genuine characters to emerge from scouting, the neighborhood was better off being able to account for so much of a teenager's time.

Finally, *college contributes to success in life*. College was important, and not just for tax purposes. It kept the family together by markedly delaying independence. It allowed for the realization of potentialities. It got young women out of town.

If mystic poet Novalis is right and "philosophy is really nostalgia, the desire to be at home"—well, then Americans have stuck pretty close to the neighborhood. In other places, there is a thing called "tradition" that tethers each generation to something lasting. This helps with things like identity, diet, aging, and maybe even equanimity. Tradition is immediately evident in Europe. Italians have Verdi on their currency. In Austria, Mozart candies always are at hand. There is no one around today who remembers sitting down to a *caffé mocha* with either of these masters, despite what some Italians may claim, so this sort of national reverence and glistening esteem are *tradition*. Yet Americans have never been able to muster support for Stephen Foster's portrait on a Heath Bar wrapper, or for a John Singer Sargent twenty-dollar bill.

The American sense of history stretches back only a few decades, so there really is no need to recall former glories. In Kraków, they have the tradition of the majestic Polish cavalry—in Alexandria, dynastic antiquity. Yucatán knows it was once Mayan, Norway used to be Viking, and there is strong evidence that Iran remembers lots about Persia. Here, however, achievement and notoriety have the same basic effect and are indistinguishable. Nostalgia pours into the American version of tradition and homogenizes.

Nostalgia pulled hard on mid-century America. Great commonalities were hauled along in powerful ways, especially by television, so much so that there is a waning, though confirmed, nostalgia for life before television. It's just plain silly trying to imagine the *television era* imparting a timeless view of the cosmos—something like *Leave It to Shiva*.

It may be that happiness and its all-out pursuit are fundamental to Americans. Europeans have insisted this is the result of Americans being chronically unhappy. There is a built-in accumulating sadness to the New World, they say, like innumerable skeletons piled up on traditional myths of faraway immigrant homelands. Americans are content to have the strong pull of just the recent past. It's all one can handle. Besides, it makes the future all the more inviting. So those in this country live like the flu virus, through adaptation. Adaptation leaves tradition behind to embrace the prevailing operational nostalgia.

At some critical point, national glory was thought to be most enjoyable when recreated regularly. America abandoned notions of time-honored cultural tradition in favor of the Hall of Fame. The Hall of Fame is unique to America; it is out of time. Tradition seems rather like a lot of signposts to ghost towns, but the Hall of Fame is for all who are revered, all who are exceptional in some American way. There really is no distinction as to *which* hall of fame, or hall of fame *for what?* The Munchkins have one. America is willing to establish the Hall of Fame in any field as a center of gravity to keep things spinning.

Nostalgia may be artificial, but it's harmless enough so long as we don't get disoriented and, by grievous misstep, vote Georgia O'Keeffe into the Shrine of Modern Pioneering Existential Abstract Representational Surrealist Post-Dada Prairie Dolls. Like any of us, she packed and unpacked her mental trunk from time to time, so as to take the edge off missing New York.

CHAPTER FOUR

Bebop Doo-wop

At first, I didn't know what to call it.
— Dizzy Gillespie

MODERN IN CONCEPTION, subways are studios mixing movement with monotony. Subways allow travelers perfect anonymity in isolated thought, free choice to reach out to any corner of a great city. Metaphysics of the "underground" plays with time and sound on short jaunts to altered states of consciousness. The subway offers freedom and escape and cover with which to move unseen beneath the streets on schizoid journeys to uncertain destinations parallel with rhythms of well-lighted routines on the surface. Underground rapid transit has only one class; everyone endures, ignores, comforts, understands, heals, and provokes everyone else. One class—humanity. In the fifties, American anti-romantic-intellectual-revolutionary spirit lived in subways. The underground message in the fifties embraced art, especially incomprehensible modern art and incomprehensible sounds.

Music seemed to have the strongest pull on this underground spirit. Music is abstract, and that was cool. It lends itself nicely to poetry, and it brought a poetic message. Like all the arts, as long as you don't charge admission there's no question of validity. From the New York subway, it was possible to find the hot jazz of *bebop* in a hundred rooms on the East and West Side, and dig some a cappella street corner quartet in doorways down Flatbush or Belmont on the way home. This music of the fifties was meant for dimly-lit dens where the mind is easily taken away, and it was just as inviting outside at twilight.

True radical thought, oddly, was not so common. There really was no lost generation of the kind Gertrude Stein had described when she borrowed the phrase of a French hotelier. Everyone could account for his or her whereabouts between the ages of twenty-five and forty. Those who preferred to remain "lost" became identified as the "beat generation," a nascent literary movement with a strong influence on American subculture.

In American cities every rail station looked alike—from Baltimore to Des Moines, to Denver and on to LA—which Jack Kerouac called "the end of America." Hitting the train station at dawn, seeing nothing but the wasted side of a city with the drunk and destitute panhandling in the gray light gave him an empty feeling. This beat generation preferred night to day, conversation to work, sex to conversation, the road to the city, the subway to the car, and anyplace to home. The beat generation may have been a right-of-passage. Some passed through it more quickly than others.

The fifties were also the decade of the cartoon, and the cartoon of the beat generation was the "beatnik." Beatniks were an amalgam of styles, typically adopting the dress of the Marseilles longshoreman (including beret and striped pullover), a taste for hors-d'oeuvres and tea or *vin extraordinaire*, and facial hair of virtually any configuration between nose and neck. Their politics tended toward anarchism but left room for certain creature comforts. The distaff version was the "beatchik"—similar in most respects but usually with less facial hair, and she could dance.

Beatniks allowed themselves to be drawn rather easily into quiet, conventional settings and seemed content to be seen as trendsetters of the lunatic fringe. On average they were comfortable with some means of support that allowed the appearance of free thought and eccentricity. They were more suburban than city but, while drawing life from the city, they played to the suburban mentality. It was reassuring to have a few beatniks close by, and a treat to be among a small group of them in the coffeehouses and out-of-the-way bars where they gathered to read apocalyptic poetry punctuated by bongo drums or an alto flute. There was shared anonymity among these intellectual habitués of the darker side.

The Beat crowd served as interpreters of Allen Ginsberg to the middle-class masses. They cheerfully condemned the society they saw—the vandals, the sybarites, and the philistines—in short, most of us. In hundreds of venues across the country, with names like "The Place Where Louie Dwells" in Washington DC, a town particularly hospitable to beatniks and sybarites alike, the applause could be heard in the finger-snapping with hands raised high, and complete agreement that the particular cat on stage was very heavy, real gone.

While education historically has occupied the American mind, organizing philosophical thought into recognizable schools has been a shortcoming. Americans have not been given credit for constructing perceptions of reality according to classical rules. In 1835 Alexis de Tocqueville went so far as to say he knew of no country in the civilized world that paid less attention to philosophical schools of their own or cared so little for what Europe had contributed.

This charge finally must be answered. Lest the world think that the playful American fifties gave no serious thought to developing a world view, certain proofs must be cited. It's true that American teleology was less formal. Nevertheless, original and substantive contributions went a long way toward defining the American philosophical proposition. In the first case, a unified theory was posited by the ultra-sophisticated writer, actor, and experimental comedian, Ernie Kovacs, in what (to satisfy Tocqueville and his ilk) might be called the "School of the Cynical Constructivism." Like all sound philosophers, Kovacs saw the world of the fifties and sixties dispassionately, and his detachment allowed for graceful maneuvering in its spontaneity and hipness.

Without even invoking that great master of reductivist thinking from the thirties, Will Rogers, there are still others. No single American philosophical school looms larger than the "Nihilistic Phenomenology" of Sid Caesar, pioneer of live television and motive force behind the era's *Your Show of Shows*. Through deft linguistic invention, he was able to demonstrate irrefutably those principles that have since evolved into the universal mainstream movement for situational ethics. His most effective vehicle was the persona of saxophonist Progress Hornsby.

These were the days musicians were talking about *rebop*, that combination of jazz and swing that happened sometime after the War—between the ornithology period of Charlie "Bird" Parker and the arrival by way of Juilliard of a trumpet player he worked with from St. Louis, Miles Davis. A quiet man of the piano, Thelonius Monk, teamed up with outrageous extrovert Dizzy Gillespie, the trumpeter kicked off Cab Calloway's band for misbehavior. Monk and Dizzy had previously formed the center of gravity for many well-known players of the forties and fifties. It was often so informal and inviting an atmosphere as to encourage the young and truly incompetent to sit in. The two would begin such an intricate and unusual progression of jazz improvisation, what critics and public alike sometimes called "Chinese jazz," that the pretenders would quickly pack up and sneak out the side exit.

Unfamiliar offbeats and accents took on a character of bop and rebop, so as to make it difficult for the unschooled listener to make any sense of it. Before long, Dizzy began to sing an occasional vocal break. This became *bebop*.

At that time, swing bands were disbanding. The new sound was in smaller groups—quartets, quintets, sextets, septets—many organized and kept alive by the alluring solo work of celebrated sidemen. The bop movement was also paralleled by a revival of Dixieland jazz of the King Oliver style from the 1920s. Incredibly, while the high priest of modernism, Dizzy Gillespie, was moving everyone gradually to bop and beyond, more Dixieland combos were formed than during any comparable period. There was something called the "Cool School," whose major laid-back, soft-spoken exponent was Lester Young, alumnus of the Count Basie band. A string of saxophone luminaries followed Young:

Sonny Stitt, Paul Desmond, Art Pepper, Zoot Sims, Yusef Lateef, and the undisputed master of the tenor sax then and thereafter, Stan Getz.

As bebop had to accommodate the curiosities of American popular nostalgia and a feverish reprise of Dixieland jazz—*rock and roll*, born of rhythm and blues and its murky roots in Southern gospel singing, arrived as a more middle-of-the-road phenomenon. It appeared as four- and five-part harmony singing that seemed to owe something to the barbershop quartets of the 1890s. For the very young of marginal sophistication, the sound was *doo-wop*, characterized by its prominent bass, falsetto descants, heavy backbeat, and a virtual absence of intelligible lyric.

Doo-wop was the music by which young Americans pursued the mundane trials of living: school, homework, washing the car, personal hygiene. It was possible to count down the Fast Forty on the popular charts and never leave the cities of New York, Chicago, Philadelphia, or the key of E-flat. Music had come to provide a kind of joy in homeostasis with the central sentiment being "the sun also sets." Rock and roll, and especially doo-wop, continually reminded teenagers that twilight time was approaching. Yet words to these songs offered a total lack of anything serious to do with twilight when it finally got here.

There had, of course, never before been anything like the *teenager*. The closest thing would have been adolescence, the juvenile stage between pupa and adult occurring in the twentieth century. Teenagers were not so much unpredictable as unsavory. Inaction, therefore, was encouraged and seen as the best way to help everybody through it. A strategy of containment centered on the high school and high school life. Boredom was suggested by parents as a pretty good approach; doo-wop supported boredom. Doo-wop, though it was also an improvisational sound of urban high energy, was like a tranquilizer by the time it reached the airways.

What fueled the tremendous ascendance of doo-wop for the ten years of its classical era were the twin magical forces of supply and demand or, more in the temper of the times, affluence and indulgence. A brash industry of mushrooming independent labels caught the shortfall of the majors, who just could not scale up fast enough for teen subculture demand.

Doo-wop was the popular expression of a lot of this reversal. Hard to define, it nevertheless was impossible to miss. At its core, doo-wop is a style of vocal music, which means its elements may be reduced to technique. Anything conceivably can be rendered in doo-wop style. However, there is a complex of these features, each one necessary, on which doo-wop leans, and it turns out these qualities appear together nowhere else in music.

First, there is group harmony, which is close and tightly figured. There is then a range of vocal parts that includes unexpected but complementary melodies and counter-rhythms. This follows a straightforward beat but with an accent on the backbeats *two* and *four*. Then, there is some instrumentation, only as cushion for the harmony or embroidery for the vocal line.

The music must also be simple and the lyric—well, it has to be trivial. The best doo-wop gives an experience that is soothing for a bit and then—*surprise*—like moving the fingers down a length of satin cord and all of a sudden there's a diamond…*dooooo-WOP—ooooo-EE—shaaaaa-BOOM*.

There certainly were Satins, there were Diamonds, too. The combination of small, independent labels meeting growing demand for doo-wop, together with the natural history of doo-wop groups, which above all was short, meant group names came and went quickly. Naming, it has been claimed, showed clear and evident patterns. Expensive dress materials had sustained popularity as a source of names—from Velvetones, to Brocades and Chiffons. Beginning in the 1940s, groups had taken on an affinity for birds. Long before The Byrds—Skylarks, Swans, Peacocks, Penguins, and Starlings all debuted. Besides the Diamonds, gemstone groups included Crystals, Emeralds, The Fabulous Pearls, even the Zircons—and, of course, The Jewels. Blossoming doo-wop groups began with the Carnations in 1952, and Daffodils, Orchids, Tiger Lillies, Roses, and Lavenders followed.

Nothing, though, was more American, more desirable, or more expressive of hormones than cars. General Motors names had a better run of it: the Bonnevilles, Fleetwoods, Belairs, Skylarks (not an encore but a different category), and Cadillacs are all easier to find on the shelves today than the Montereys, Coronets, or The Studebaker 7.

Through indulgence and teen idolatry, the industry focus was on the high school. This was the first and last time the place has been able to endure the glare of the spotlight. As for doo-wop groups, although most didn't actually start out on street corners, it is entirely in keeping with the teen aspect of the genre that nearly all these groups ended up there.

Sexual power of the age tongue-tied the lyricist, which brings us to the final quality of the doo-wop style: nonsense. Nonsense syllables expressed the preference for communicating something primeval over saying anything that might possibly lead to ridicule or humiliation. Any syllable at all would keep the time and float the harmony. Questions were, of course, just as metaphysical as ever: what is it, where is it, who put it there? There were, however, new and plaintive ways of expressing the *shing-a-ling-a-ling* and *ka-dang* of first love. After many years, there emerged the sense that "it's in his kiss," but there has never been a satisfactory answer to "who put the bop?" The grammar of doo-wop nonsense is, very simply, incantation and release: *Bom ba-ba bom, day-doo ron ron-ron, rama-lama ding-dong, dit da-dit da-dit, shoo dooten shooby doo, ding-a-dong ding Blue Moon*. The Laurels eventually hammered home the obvious with their tune titled, "Baby Talk."

Popular music generally resists categorization, and it necessarily comes and goes. By 1964 the Beatles were in full voice, brushing only briefly the coat tails of neo-doo-wop style. Purity of musical elements had had their day with running bass, castrato top end, nonsense harmony, group echoes of the lead, heavy backbeat, and the trailing falsetto—all to the accompaniment of only snapping fingers and clapping hands.

Each new sound breaks taxonomy the instant it becomes noticed. Doo-wop originated in a moment when there were no instruments; voices had to make all the sounds. Bebop, at about the same moment, was all instruments and used no voice until Dizzy started to hum his scat nonsense out loud. Music was fascinating and accessible to the emotional amateur and sexual dilettante. Memory brings it cascading from above, traveling up stairwells, over rooftops, out from the corners of buildings, running down underground into urban subway echo chambers. Subways are studios, home to unintelligible jazz and arcane pop harmony, the sacred tomb of the lost chord.

CHAPTER FIVE

Dreams of Disaster

*Somewhere between the gradual extinction of human
liberty and the total extinction of terrestrial life...*
— Ursula K. LeGuin

JUST ABOVE THE REPTILIAN brain stem is a spot in all humans that seeks out the threatening, the ominous, and the scary. A corollary to instinctual aggression, it is the attraction of similar intensity to vulnerability and helplessness. Once frightened out of their wits, human beings are somehow more comfortable with their surroundings, back in touch with the primal forces and, all in all, better prepared for what's coming. The world is a fragile place. There truly is ruin and desolation at every turn. In such a dangerous region, all organisms, it seems, periodically look to terrify themselves, thereby moving back toward equilibrium. Complacency is the real hazard here, so there are good reasons for peering into dark places.

Some things horrify everybody and are extremely popular for it: suffocation, zombies, alien botany, Joan Crawford. Each generation institutionalizes its contemplation of the unthinkable. The atomic era, commencing in 1945, revitalized a long run with science fiction. This was the start of late-twentieth-century mass memory, the popular misunderstanding of technology and all hallucinations up to and including alien abduction.

The true beginnings might logically be placed with Jules Verne and his fantastic visions from the nineteenth century, but one might just as well go back to the homunculus legends of the middle ages. In the post-war decade there was widespread and personal involvement with science fiction. Later on, there was something called "science fantasy," the distinction being only in the degree to which one incorporates popular notions of physics—fantasy implying more weight being given to a rather undisciplined imagination.

Science fiction has never reached the level of popularity some enthusiasts might suggest—never really broken out from cult status. Resolving problems Nature brings, all with doom immanent and the clock ticking, is an idea with lasting appeal. The material for science fiction comes from a number of literary sources. In some cultures, it tends to concentrate on a peculiar, usually weird or morally questionable, aspect of humanity. Human experimentation, the quest for the perfect power source, and assorted mutations are enduring subjects. American science fiction lacks the intensity and drama of most European versions, and although the stakes are always higher in terms of sheer numbers of lives lost and replacement values of damages sustained, Americans have tended to be quite a bit less cerebral about it. This comes principally from two elemental influences: (1) American enjoyment of science fiction demands a logical explanation for nearly everything within the attention span, and (2) behind every tight situation is that critical mistake of, once again, tampering with life forces. With countless visions of death and destruction comes the concluding apologia, *there are some things humans are not meant to know*.... Science repeatedly runs amok through stupidity, arrogance, its silly conventions, or the epistemological avarice of having to *know* everything. After all, in 1945 science and American (that is to say, German) scientists had pushed back the frontiers, and whether it was *harnessing* or *unleashing* (we never really got it straight) a terrible force, everyone was unclear about what this meant to the old rules for scientific conduct. The consequences were, of course, a fantastic realm for speculation.

Science's part in all this was that it had created it—accidentally. Sometimes science realized it. This saved Earth, but usually was not enough to save the story. Far too often, to the delight of many, science was up against it, opposing no less than the embodiment of all evil. *Science*, of course, was represented on the page or in the movie house as a graying Buddhist republican, standing five feet six inches tall, quoting Lao-Tsu or Mr. Jefferson and representing not only the most microbiology, stereochemistry and quantum theory that can be crammed into one head but the very best of humanity. *Science* had a ravishing daughter (*Young America*) whose size-two wardrobe was one revealing size too small.

This was not the science fiction of Edgar Allen Poe that Baudelaire so admired: transmigration of souls, hundred-year-old opium addicts, speculative physics, and galactic ballooning. Tastes were running to life forces in the atomic age and, with the comic book as its literary source, stories moved easily to the motion picture screen. Extra-terrestrials, mutants, consolidated creatures, amalgamated beasts, the gargantuan, the aggressive, the smelly and maladaptive, leviathans ingesting small cities—all were utterly without conscience and hell-bent on a good time ashore, usually in New York. Hollywood knew the public would like the thrilling, cinematic potential of the bomb long before the public knew it. But there are only so many ways you can drop the bomb.

In the end, science was ill-equipped to handle the inevitable bedlam. Something better, well-fed, and undefeated was found in the military. The army was greater than science, as can be continuously observed in what occupies bright young graduate physicists and the better part of NASA's budget. Monsters actually became gradually less interesting, not so much an intriguing menace now as boisterous and ill-bred. When the throng was in a swivet over some irradiated gorgon, soldiers stemmed the tide of destruction. Themes became more of a caricature, using titles beginning with *Attack of the …*, or the more immediate, *Invasion of the …*, clearly drawing the story along two dimensions—black and white. What often happened was the military's subduing the monster by using the bomb, against the better judgment of the young scientist. It all obscured and camouflaged the nuclear horizon for some time.

Science fiction films went almost immediately to television, where something else was going on. For many years, *Captain Video* explored science fiction ideas in a television format and there was the much more successful science fictional *Dr. Who* series from the BBC. For the most part, television slept, and the dreams television dreamed served another critical purpose at the heart of national security: domestic tranquility.

Women, it was noticed, had been running the country. In charge of every aspect of life at home, women had operated the factories that won the war. A changing order was evident, hopelessly bereft of any workable model. The structure of domestic living needed modification, new techniques—just to get along. Too many hot rivets had been slung, too many manifolds assembled. Society demanded an appropriate response, and finally, it arrived. It was known as the "situation comedy." Just back from the brink of destruction, the real concern was a precarious notion of security. Security was actually so important that dullness and general inactivity were preferred. The situation comedy provided a reflection of the new order and quickly succeeded in restoring domestic life by exhibiting the concept of uniform, reassuring predictability.

The mark of this form was to produce outlandish circumstances in the uneventful home. Reassurance came with seeing the incredible unfold amid unshakable calm. Factories were retooling and there were "domestic aids" available in a vast array of products. The new domestic scene had literally been manufactured, a consumer economy emerging from those American factories, changed forever by the strange feminine hands that had filled in for four years.

The unthinkable is, as everyone knows, irresistible. Science fiction moved from a tease to something important. The something that emerged soon became too large for science fiction to handle and its dimensions were recognized as better suited to drama—drama on a new scale. What we stumbled upon by mixing cartoons, politics, world war, domestic security, and the lack of somewhere for science fiction to go was back to this apocalyptic vision. Our recreation became modern variations on the *end of the world—no, really!* Atomic fallout was raining into the cinema now. This inability to resist the imponderable was the subject for film and, therefore, the current mode for science fiction. Science fiction did something new. The wholly unanticipated sequel to having made the world free and come out of it so handsomely, was to assume responsibility. This, not for even the merest hope of improving any part of it but for the seemingly likely possibility of screwing up on a grander scale than had been imaginable before now.

For purposes of trying to come to terms with any of this, *On the Beach* is perhaps the best survivor, certainly one of the best attempts at a complete vision—and one with many imitators. It offered the chance to savor the full flavor and mood of utter atomic destruction on a planetary scale. Probably too intense for Americans, even now, even in L.A.—it is actually Australian radio which gives the news. Lethal radioactivity had already done in the rest of humanity, so it was just as well that Americans, having been responsible for it, did not survive to face the stunned and unforgiving next of kin. Walking the beach, the players imagine that it is a dream, while inevitably they are brought back to growing sickness and despair. *On the Beach* finished off the decade with a whimper as a general comment on the Sputnik business and the impression that things may be moving pretty fast. Not discounting *Dr. Strangelove* in 1963, the utterly humorless depictions in *On the Beach* nicely summarized the willowy substructure of survival.

The romp through spacescapes and back lots of science fiction brought us to the predominating quality of the times. Science fiction was a way to redraw the lines from time to time, change the rules and run different ideas through hypothetical social experiments. The need to redefine where everyone was going injected a fair quantity of science fiction residue into the process.

Dangers of newly acquired knowledge were recognized by others as well. The Russian film of the period, *Nine Days in One Year* provided an orientation of accidental existentialism. Other versions of the true horrors of the nuclear age and ultimate doom emerged in England and France while the Japanese, for reasons one can guess, stuck with monsters.

In the late fifties, the social order recognized it was being threatened. The world had proven, after all, to be quite fragile, and large parts of it could now be altered very quickly. With the kind of devastation Americans had brought, it was just prudent to draw the wagons around the campfire, shore up where we could, and try to minimize disorganization. Definitions of family were not going to reach any high-water marks. Instead, well-adjusted children would be prepared for the technological challenges to come. The twilight sleep all enjoyed in accepting these methods of social preservation was induced by the scopolamine of sci-tech victory over worldly evil. There wasn't too much more thinking to be done on the subject. Science was in the American military and that was the place for it.

The community's part was civil defense, a theoretical technique for survival from the radiation stockpiled in those deadly warheads produced so as to keep the population secure. The idea of civil defense was largely social. Neighbors building their own private shelters tended to be the type least likely to be chosen by Professor Quatermass to wait out doomsday and begin the new civilization after the smoke cleared. How depressing it was to imagine institutions of the future designed solely by the ultra-paranoid and hyper-greedy. Still, this method promised to preserve the essentials of sexual predestination, scholastic utilitarianism, and national morality—and someone had to do the digging.

Survival became important. It no longer was assured. Human genius that created the "peaceful uses of the atom" had also destroyed innocence and purity, and had taken a real shot at goodness. Mechanistic science had taken the quantum leap, and there was no discernible line separating science fiction and science. Fantastic utopias, parallel universes, the ravaging subterranean morlocks, and even the ecstasy of discovery had all been scattered by the anodizing aftermath of the bomb. If equanimity could not be retrieved, it would be constructed so no one would notice the difference.

2

BOOK OF HERESIES

Recollecting decades of the sixties and seventies...

Preoccupations embraced mystical transformations, personal power, and the problem of leisure.

Staring into the magic of social progress, science, and technology, there was the search for secret knowledge.

The black American's legacy is a struggle of two souls and the Third World. Racism makes war's case.

A succession of careers forms a complete life only recognizable when it is done, having made and re-made itself.

In silent ecstasies, mutual confusion intrudes—discouraging, neglecting, and destroying smart women.

CHAPTER SIX

Letter to Abigail

*Guard well your spare moments.
They are like uncut diamonds.*
— Ralph Waldo Emerson

LEISURE HAS LOST THE best part of its original meaning. To reclaim some sense of what it is supposed to be, many define leisure in terms of time. This merely increases the burden. Time is allocated in much the same way it is accounted for. From social economists with too much of it on their hands, many have come to think about leisure time as a commodity to be used up, consumed, either by doing something with it or by doing nothing. A brief (if not altogether leisurely) stroll through the last millennium suggests that, instead of increasing productivity to meet human needs, piling up leisure time moves one in the opposite direction. What is the revitalizing human occupation in leisure?

Aspirations for the next generation, and the next after them, seem to include the desire that they have the chance to put every moment to better use. Somehow, these children will have good judgment and blissful moments—replacing mischief, loathing, idleness, and greed with all things creative, restorative, and sublime. Both hope and guilt may be behind the wish that succeeding generations will make a better accounting of themselves.

The curious truth is that ideas of leisure tend always to be projected into future generations. The Greek abstraction of leisure, that one is free to exercise the full use of one's powers along the lines of excellence, seems far too potent and overwhelming. Now leisure is simply freedom, opportunity, exemption from toil. Leisure full-strength needs to be diluted with several parts squandering, thoughtless mismanagement, and inferior pursuits.

Generations to come will have to find better ways to spend their time in the name of greater satisfaction and a sense of wellbeing. Then how should these surroundings be prepared so that others will construct temples of awesome beauty?

Hindu and Sanskrit traditions, with their strict adherence to caste duties, pointed the way to acceptance of *karma*—that is, action. One's present station is the result of the sum of all deeds and thoughts of all former existence. In the ancient *Bhagavad Gita*, young archer Arjuna sees his princely duty in reconciliation of the discipline of the mind with the necessity for physical action. The eternal process applies to the present and determines in what form the soul transmigrates. Men thus were compelled to follow a trade or profession—a priest, a merchant, a warrior, or stoker of the fires at the public baths. He was bound by the calling of his father and his father's father, and not free to circulate at higher grades of life. Simple rebirth, if this is ever simple, means the opportunity to improve the world of the living.

Reincarnation is a little more complicated. As *metempsychosis*, transmigration of the soul conveys the idea of passage from one human or animal body to another. Life, in all cases, is preparation for life to come. For the Buddhist there is a succession of incarnations. In Zen and ancient Jainism there comes a moment of sudden awakening to one's bondage, *satori*, that gets one free of it. If the moral-religious *Laws of Manu* from 200 BC obtain in how time is allotted, then the succession of finite births of the immutable soul constitutes humanity's stream of second chances.

> *I must study politics and war that my sons may have the liberty to study mathematics and philosophy.*

None of John Adams' Sanskrit writings survive. However, these lines in English from his letter to Abigail Adams in the spring of 1781 demonstrate faith in princely duty, the transmigration of the soul, progression to higher vision and wiser thought, the renunciation of worldly necessity, and the insignificance of nearly everything else. Here is the universal principle that there are just not enough hours in the day. Yet there is the impulse to leave behind a better world than this one.

The America of John Adams was an invention of his own times and his fellow conspirators. They faced much nasty duty, and their legacy was less a completed work than an atmosphere in which something virtuous would one day thrive. For example, there was no pretense to democracy then. What is sometimes called "pure democracy" was never intended. Instead, these men (women, alas, did not vote on it) set up a republic in recognition that the young country even then was too dispersed and culturally too diverse to function if every enfranchised citizen was encouraged to participate directly in government.

Many rights thought constitutional today are not found in the Constitution. Education, personal autonomy, separation of church and state, judicial review, and free enterprise are each from time to time declared fundamental to the American system and said to be the basis of the first generation's legacy. Not one of these phrases appears in the Constitution.

The framers basically set limits on government and provided the political majority the means to act on social topics, if it was so inclined. The Constitution neither grants, nor does it insist upon, an affirmative right to education. The chances of government interfering in personal autonomy were thought so remote as not to be worth mentioning. Limited government, they thought, would be incapable of abusing individual rights.

Early on, many states favored a particular religion: Anglicanism in the South and Congregationalism (American Shinto) in the North. This went on until diehard Massachusetts finally abandoned state-favored religion in 1833.

Likewise, judicial review seems to be an American anomaly. It was as unforeseen by the founders as it is unthinkable in virtually every other country. There is scant appeal in a small band of judges, whose independence and power grow solely from the circumstance that they never have to face the voters, immersing itself in the rights of every autonomous individual. There is every chance the rascals will frustrate the will of a democratically-elected legislature.

The times of John Adams and his fellows were filled with hope but caution. Leisure as exemption from toil meant Adams could abandon his study of war. In the hundred years that followed Adams's death (and Jefferson at Monticello later that same afternoon), the lifespan of Americans doubled as the occupational workload was cut in half. Adams had witnessed a war-weary world exile Napoleon to St. Helena. He imagined scientific genius and material progress would follow.

A century after Adams, the German Emperor was sailing at his leisure on the Baltic Sea. A launch flying the Kaiser's colors hurriedly approached with urgent news from the Balkan Peninsula that the heir to the Austrian throne had been assassinated. All peaceful momentum of the nineteenth century suddenly was lost in a moment that made war an international industry.

Spurious aspects of preparing for war have been pointed out by generations of military pupils at Sandhurst and Saint-Cyr, whose knowledge of war remains theoretical, anticipatory, and secondhand. All logic of war seems to break down at the moment action commences. One needs some modifying principle to govern aggression and render it in some way bounded.

A report to Adams today might elaborate on the passing of war and the closing up of the yawning space between metaphysicians and politicians. War, it might be ventured, will actually pass away due to humans no longer being fit for its stresses. It just can't be prosecuted with so little conviction.

War, Mr. Adams, is hyperbole and overstatement. If aggression is logical nonsense, then war, as Dickens might put it, is "nonsense on stilts."

Whether it be extreme intimacy or extreme enmity, war is extremity. It is the extremity of ignoring another's presence by absorbing him so that he disappears. Perpetual tantrum, war neither satisfies nor knows its end. Can it be that war is the only human act that can have no purpose? One might conclude that war is none other than a brief respite from thinking.

> I must study politics and war that my sons may have the liberty to study mathematics and philosophy. My sons ought to study mathematics and philosophy, geography, natural history, naval architecture, navigation, commerce and agriculture....

Sons are sometimes drawn to the interests of the father. John Quincy Adams was more inclined to study politics than painting. There may be less rather than more philosophy in a succeeding generation, but this does not mute the desire to pass the baton upward and see the soul evolve according to the principle of better use of time.

It is difficult for most to concentrate on a multitude of things in only a single lifetime; those who can and do are deemed extraordinary. Yet the evolutionary process is surest perhaps in the lives of such individuals who can combine occupation and leisure in more or less equal measure during their spans. John Adams lived nearly thirty years after his 1797 inaugural at age sixty-one. Jefferson, then Madison, had similarly ample stretches of state-mandated leisure.

Belief in the evolution of the soul being revealed in the longevity of the gifted is an inviting idea.

Adams pointed toward a purpose for the American soul. The natural state for all of us, he said, springs from honest judgments and enlightened hearts, rather than descending from ancient accidents. Adams wanted us to neglect our own impossibilities. We should, he thought, be wholly inattentive to the inevitability of failure. America should be filled with sanguine knowledge and an excess of virtue. Leisure is prodded by elevated ideas and high destinies.

Yet for every philosopher there is somewhere a bailiff. The nation of John Adams was all possibility. A courier could ride from the seat of government to the frontier in a single day. The presidential address to the average yahoo in America at the beginning of the twentieth century was quite different.

Almost no one claims to remember a time when this human burden of *doing* and of *being* was easy. Time is indeed the rarest commodity, and thinking too much about how best to use it makes everybody nervous. Time cannot be stored or saved or produced at a rate greater than it is used up. The well-to-do and the clever have no more of it than the poor and the confused. There is, therefore, a great attraction to idleness in the modern world.

Idleness takes time. It creates a space that then can be filled with leisure. This modern sentiment was noted more than a century ago when a novelist admitted to a hope that succeeding generations would be able to be idle. Idleness would allow us to rest by the sea and dream—to dance and enjoy the beauty of a beautiful world. How glorious it is, so the Spanish proverb goes, "to do nothing and rest afterward."

Or there is the French view revealed by cinema director Jean Renoir that "the foundation of all civilization is loitering—without open spaces, there is no movement."

Maybe modern thought really began in the Bronze Age. This is when the elevated idea of an evolving human soul first appeared. Aquinas saw the merit of this and tried to simplify his view in four thousand pages of the *Summa Theologiæ*, proving how theology, or knowledge of God, was the object of the soul's journey. Some commentators of the *Gita* say its first six chapters are concerned with knowledge of the soul—and the next six, with knowledge of theology. Saint Thomas, of course, cited Augustine and not Arjuna.

> *I must study politics and war that my sons may have the liberty to study mathematics and philosophy. My sons ought to study mathematics and philosophy, geography, natural history, naval architecture, navigation, commerce and agriculture, in order to give their children a right to study painting, poetry, music, architecture, statuary, tapestry and porcelain.*

John's letter to Abigail is a confession that each must advance to a higher state and, there, know wiser uses of one's allotted time. This pulls across generations even as echoes of the Sanskrit reveal the irony that only so much can come from good things, that morality must share the stage with action. For colonial Americans, this meant things of the soul were to come only after the land had been cleared and enemies slain. The great trick, as Adams may have been hinting, is for humankind to run out of enemies and find the soul, all in the same generation.

Leonardo da Vinci has been offered up as proof for many that humankind is capable of spending time creating beauty, following the soul on its upward journey. Yet he earned his keep in weapons design, fashioning armaments for his patrons from Milan to the Loire Valley. No one was more imaginative in advancing the art of war. But peace broke out often, and this genius of many centuries turned to the plastic and graphic arts, for which he is best remembered. Only when war and its excitements were finished did Leonardo embrace the sublime.

CHAPTER SEVEN

Ordinary Alchemy

And we are magic talking to itself, noisy and alone.
— Anne Sexton

Americans looked upon many mid-century marvels of transformation. Space had been penetrated, and in 1960 there were seventeen satellites around the planet. Solid state electronics with its "micro-miniature" transistors had made possible the electronic brains that could compute, coordinate, control, and remember virtually anything asked of them. Hydrogen fission had arrived, even a portable fuel cell. Salty sea water could be converted to fresh water. Jonas Salk and Albert Sabin had helped to bring under control polio, the scourge of infantile paralysis. Skin, cartilage, bone, connective tissue, and major organs of the body were being stored in organ banks for use when needed—by a new host, that is. Commercial jet aviation had shrunk the world by cutting trans-Atlantic travel to seven hours. The world looked forward to manned space flights and fabulous medical cures.

Humans have difficulty distinguishing power from knowledge. For millennia, certain words, gesticulations, and pictures executed in precise ways have been thought to give humans control over nature and, most immediately, over other humans. Magic was the means, and magical secrets were sought in the most unlikely surroundings. Television manipulated words and gesticulations, and by 1961 world wire services were transmitting ten million words a day. There was plenty of potentially powerful magic to choose from, and the way in which science of the time was being reported lent a circus atmosphere to events of the day, encouraging everyone to discover the magic that would give them their own personal power.

Not that there was anything unusual or particularly modern in the mass-pursuit of secret knowledge. It's the kind of shortcut to fulfillment that always has been attractive. A century before Copernicus published the book he had been working on for some thirty years about the revolution of planets, the Medici family of Florence had begun putting together a library of Greek works that had not yet been translated into Latin. Cosimo de Medici's merchants were sent out to compete with, meaning outbid, scholars of the West, who themselves were bringing back literary treasures from Asia Minor.

Among the books delivered to Medici were the *Dialogues* of Plato but what caught his eye was an incomplete manuscript of the *Corpus Hermeticum*, that fabulous book of Middle Ages magic. His secretary, Ficino, had already begun translating the *Dialogues* when Cosimo asked him to get started on the *Corpus Hermeticum*—for he must have this esoteric knowledge. Cosimo died in the next year, 1464, long before the books of magic were shown to be fakes. Fakery was not the most serious of crimes. In fact, fakery in connection with magic can be seen as helpful, concealing the real power by allowing the bogus artifacts and sleights-of-hand to be found out. "Knowledge is power" was not actually written down until Francis Bacon put it in his preamble to the *Novum Organum* of 1620. Nonetheless, there is a simple joy, as one imagines Ficino to have felt, that comes from a sense that the world is awesomely beautiful but understandable, and there is a transcendent way in which it should be experienced.

An intermingling of belief focused itself in the great city of Alexandria just at the beginnings of a wave of new science and toward the close of the pre-Christian era. Rapid advances in science have often been accompanied by a popular appeal of abstract disciplines and a spirited return to contemplating natural forces.

The art of alchemy sprang from dim and distant origins, re-igniting the search for the grand *arcanum* that Ptolemaic Greek and Egyptian philosophers thought of as the extract of "vital nature." Too many intervening years and several nervous Roman emperors had destroyed what texts on the subject of alchemy existed before the current era, but it doesn't seem to matter. There are plenty of examples of the practice in every century. Burning books always heightens curiosity, and few things are more attractive than secret knowledge—knowing that it is to be revealed only to the very few.

As for alchemy itself as both art and philosophy, if its beginning was once obscure, it was now opaque. An Egyptian sage and legendary "adept," as they called alchemists who knew what they were doing, is credited with a tome he called the *Chema*, which was thought to have provided the root of the word, alchemy. Greeks, on the other hand, called molten metals, poured or cast as ingot, *chyma*. Signore Ficino was learning another explanation—that the true genius of alchemy was the inventor of that magic seal that made vessels airtight, *Hermes Trismegistus*—Thrice Great Hermes, priest of Egyptian legend, god of wisdom, scribe of the underworld, and Pharaoh in multitudinous forms over his reign of 3,226 years. When the Greeks appropriated Hermes Trismegistus and the hermetic seal, they deemed Hermes messenger of the gods and patron of both merchants and thieves, so as to maintain (one might suppose) the Greek notion of "stasis," or balance. He was simply too much god with too vast a dominion, and the by-product of his abduction to Hellenic life was to collect and lay down the Hermetic arts and all teachings founded on supernatural wisdom. These teachings were claimed to have been inscribed on an emerald tablet. There, according to the most authoritative sources, were recorded the principles of the grand arcanum, the ultimate secret supposed to be behind astrology, alchemy, and magic—painstakingly set forth in exceedingly cryptic instructions that somehow have been misplaced.

Faith fosters science and the occult in more or less equal measure. Certain historians have not been embarrassed to spend time re-assessing Neoplatonic magic of the Middle Ages and the renewed interest in Hermeticism in the context of the deep thinking of Renaissance Europe. Some conclude it may be the basis of modern science. Late-twentieth-century science makes plenty of room for fuzzy logic. A good deal of the logic in America in the sixties was fuzzy. In the rough and real terrain of popular intellectual magic there was a conviction of the value of personal experience and an openness to a poetic description of how things happen.

Magic must be *real*. It needs to accomplish something visible, or otherwise sensible, and cannot masquerade as merely special knowledge. Alchemy was regarded as the inductive means to participating in the union of natural and supernatural. Drifting from the physical to the spiritual is easy enough, but this can never purify either's essence to the exclusion of the other. Turning base metals into gold was the showman's vulgar spectacle, but the higher quest became the search for celestial essences—not only material riches but also spiritual wealth. Intellectual free spirits of the 1600s accepted magic on these terms: as being more closely tied to natural desire than to reasoning.

Nature ran its course, meandering along the path, and from time to time simply got distracted or too full of herself and lapsed into excess with things like two-headed snakes or purple-aqua sunsets. Just as magic is not theoretical, neither is it neutral. Usually, it is judged to be either good (that is, benign and white), or evil and pernicious black magic. It is part of the whole complex of magic that it has nearly always been hard to tell which spirits one was dealing with—divine or diabolical, magic or sorcery.

A lasting quality of magic is how well it appears to have kept up with developments in science, even as it sets itself in opposition. As more universal essences became known, magic put them into perspective. Numbers, for example, have always held magical attributes—some perfect, others unlucky or impotent. Counting with them was not thought of as their highest use. Aristotle's notion of the hierarchy of being observes lesser forms of nature reproduce by self-duplication while perfect forms are generated sexually. Sex, some young scientists of the sixties insisted, was perfect; it was all the Aristotle many of them needed.

Emergence of the *new science* of an age is tied to magic and explanations for sensible change made apparent. Alchemy keeps its seeking eye on the final cause, a task science is ill-suited to and which science abandoned shortly after it invented itself. This is one means of distinguishing magic and science, but any distinction—to say it yet one more way—is probably not worth the trouble. Science has triumphed over magic in the modern world for its explanation of the physical character of the fundamental units of nature, but this is actually the point where the alchemist begins.

Magic, transformation and the attendant rituals abounded in the sixties. The frontier and the fringe beyond had become indistinguishable with psychic phenomena: automatic writing, UFOs, ESP, lost Atlantis, extraterrestrial intelligence, and the Loch Ness Monster.

Reordering American popular thought may have begun with the adult cartoon, but it would evolve to the brown rice vegetarian, the communal house, and "the Great Subculture." It was the crush of large numbers of sixties youth that made subculture the popular version. The number of committed tribesmen and the visibly weird may not have been proportionately so great, but the overwhelming population of the crypto-hip moved through many walks of life undetected, donning their beads and feathers only on occasions of spiritual release. The number of people using marijuana regularly or who had experienced LSD was, considering its illegality, enormous. Serious embrace of the supernatural was the youthful reaction to what appeared to be a self-indulgent, complacent, silly society. Seekers of purity were bent on employing all sorts of artificial chemical substances to bring them to natural states of consciousness.

Paranoia and alchemy are extreme effects of the simple principle of change. In any age of big secrets, the paranoid style of literature has been refined. Once the unconventional anti-hero gets his bearings, she or he is able to follow the journey to redemption. Fantasies of the American individual in direct contact with the essences put each one in the presence of the arcanum and reckoned their course in the archetypal good-and-evil plane. Paranoid literature came through William Burroughs on to a fully-rendered state in Kurt Vonnegut. It is undeniably an international, rather than an American, style. Kafka, of course, knew he was being watched. The paranoid style is that peculiar psychosis that attends the elected, the self-realized, and seers of gigantic things.

The American experience has directed the ready mind in a certain way that, when blended with the principles of alchemy, diffuses paranoid tendencies. Like so many histories, American history has repeatedly confirmed the suspicion that power is a sinister and malevolent influence that at its worst is an unnatural corruption and, at best, wastes valuable time. Paranoids continue to be iconoclastic symbols who insist there is so much less in the real world than meets the mind.

Before paranoid literature there was Ben Jonson. His

great play is concerned with human, rather than elemental, alchemy. *The Alchemist* has a central image of transmutation. The play is about avarice, and the incorruptible symbol of avarice is gold. The author was a solid critic of the vice and explores the variety of ways in which human energies can be misdirected and ingenuity squandered on acquisitive pursuits. He illustrates American journalist A.J. Liebling's observation of the sixties: "If a man of sufficiently complex mind directs it in an adequately perverse way, he can succeed in kicking his own ass out the door and into the street."

In the mid-sixties, wizards of science proclaimed there was something smaller and harder to find than the electron, and that these were "sub-subatomic." They might just as well be given whimsical names of hope, with inescapable allusions to our confusion and fallibility. Quarks, then, are known by name: charmed, truth, beauty, strange.

The subculture illuminati historically have been a strong force. Personal transmutation in the service of making good things happen can be either freely published for the benefit of everyone, or it can be held close. Closely held knowledge is the tradition of the Taoist secret societies, Sufis of Islam, Zen Buddhists, and the Tantrics of India. In the West, periodically recurring ages of heresies began with the Gnostics and was carried on at the folk level with a more domesticated version of magic. The American search was for a magic that would combine and reveal the shamanistic-yogic-gnostic-socioeconomic view of humankind as a child of nature.

Still, it must have startled all of science, busy pulling knowledge apart from power, to pursue new marvels of transformation when *neuro-psycho-biochemico-cyberneticists* reminded everyone that the engine of innovation runs on abstract disciplines and a spirited return to contemplating natural forces.

CHAPTER EIGHT

Double Souls

It is easier to build strong children than to repair broken men.
— Frederick Douglass

Habits of mind often develop in complicated ways. The American mind can be lively and audacious but is, by nature, as habitual as any other. The distinguishing feature may be the speed with which minds here are made up. Americans have had so much practical experience that opinions are formed quickly. This tendency seems to apply equally to insight and prejudice, moving with dispatch in either direction.

The credo of America is an abbreviated list of recurring ideas housed in sturdy institutions but sustained by fragile conventions. Many feel the need for a new creed to serve a moral struggle, and it is important the struggle be a moral one: dramatic, serious, and with high stakes. Any American creed urges living up to numerous distinct and high principles equally. For this is the land of essential dignity but also of equality, freedom but justice, Homer Plessy and Judge Ferguson but Oliver Brown, and the Topeka Board too.

Anglos pretty generally have not taken to newcomers. They selectively forget their role as immigrant usurper of very many places. Early Anglo Americans often felt Germans and Scandinavians were insular and disdainful. Italians they considered unrefined and a bit fearsome. The Irish, well, the Irish have been questioned, detained, and shown the door on so many counts.

Prejudice involving national origin is transient and correlated with ignorance. It is usually far from comical. Yet noble ideas of the American habit remain very much the ideas of white people, with tacit and persistent exclusion of black, red, brown, and other races.

When Louis Leaky unearthed signs of human universal black heritage in the Olduvai Gorge, rediscovering Africa's covered-up ancient past, this astounding find was met with a troubled and confused response. A two-million-year-old black primogenitor was not everyone's preference for a recurring idea.

Racism is an invention. Its most popular use and purpose is in the service of dominance. Racism puts a sharp edge on the lines of separation between peoples and curiously bends back upon itself. It becomes emblematic of survival. It seeks to invent an enemy's own racism, which the racist makes himself feel. British commanders created the race of (Germanic) Huns to more convincingly berate Germans, as if redefining race were a prima facia case for their position. Nazi racism conflated race and culture and pointed critically to the American conscience, though it was still difficult to persuade black Americans in 1939.

Since their very beginnings, American habitual ideas and institutions ironically have retained their power and much of their luster for those most cruelly oppressed in the reality of everyday. Indeed, the American creed has meant much more to minority blacks than majority whites precisely for its signifying of rights unfulfilled.

Doctrinaire ravings of the Teutonic "Master Race" as a principle abetting the Second World War certainly did not eliminate American racism. Instead, the war drove it underground. America clung to its habits as it forbade Chinese, faithful allies in the war, from becoming citizens. Japanese internment camps were incorporated into the war effort, but camps for Italians were felt to be unnecessary. If there were any true gains against racial bigotry during the 1940s, it was not by challenging the majority view, rather by raising minority consciousness.

No speaker on American racism has surpassed the eloquence and poetry of W.E.B. DuBois. He observed in 1903 that the problem of the slave trade was difficult, intricate, and altogether perplexing, and that our inherited habits were based on a shameful past. Speaking of the individual man or woman as the highest achievement of any nation, he recognized that black Americans struggle to be both black and American, and this conflict stands between one side of the soul and the other, effectively splitting the black soul in two.

DuBois' basic principle was simple: no people is to be trusted with the destinies of another. During the First World War, he reflected on his popular work, *Up from Slavery*, and summarized in an unpublished essay the effect of poverty on a growing boy or girl and the will and actions taken to strive against it. He saw the great divergence of opinion about the American negro as not separated by color but by a habit of thinking. Disenfranchisement and the legal caste system that emerged after the Civil War was, in the end, discrimination against ability.

He knew the "twoness" of black people through its having two of everything: thoughts, ideals, unreconciled aspirations. DuBois described the wish to be both black and American in his *Souls of Black Folk*. It is the unique inner strife that comes out of American racism. What must be resolved is the longing to attain self-conscious personhood in one body, to blend the double soul into the truer self.

Another son of slavery had tried to disarm racism before the twentieth century, before the color line was to become the conspicuous problem in America. Frederick Augustus Washington Bailey claimed he well understood freedom through its privation; he learned this approach from Aristotle. He compounded his own white western orientation by taking a new name, a fugitive's name, based on a character from Sir Walter Scott's *Lady of the Lake*. As Frederick Douglass, the Sage of Anacostia, at age forty-seven he saw abolished what he called the greatest evil. He then moved toward his own sense of identity and destiny as an individual altogether beyond race.

Douglass was hardly rhapsodic about Africa and saw nothing wrong with former slaves taking for themselves emancipation names borrowed from white American heroes. Douglass blended his own two souls as American Minister to Haiti, having the active belief that all four million former slaves were now Americans, self-defined, and would do better to take little notice of any African identity.

Douglass met the lawyer from Illinois. He saw him elected President on a promise of no more slave states in the

Union. In his second inaugural address, President Lincoln spoke of the "peculiar and powerful interests" of slaves as the cause of the war the nation was then enduring. In the President's remarks, he described the country as having two souls, with two prayers, that rather than resolve things had created a terrible "offense." In the last few weeks before his assassination, Lincoln urged a return to the divine principles Americans recognized but had somehow forgotten.

One hundred years later, in the last few days before he was assassinated, Malcolm X asserted that the problems of blacks had ceased to be confined to the "American negro"; rather, these problems should be understood within an international context. Malcolm called this an "Allied" problem, certainly manifest in Britain, but more particularly in France and America. Even in 1939, blacks were not drafted; "they could not join the Navy." Then, when what he called the "town negro" and the "black leader" spoke up for equality in the "sweet land of liberty," the result was that many negroes were killed in combat. Which soul was it that perished, one might wonder?

The Second World War had fit rather neatly into the morality play structure Americans favored. Now there were other nations' wars in which to take part, in the manner of the ancient Celtic saying: "Is this a private fight, or can anyone get in?" Morality was once again becoming an American obsession.

In Vietnam, Americans had alternately stood as an ally of the French; trained Ho Chí Minh's guerrillas to throw grenades at the French; supported Ho against the French colonialists; supported France against Ho in the cause of

NATO, not Vietnam; and, finally, succeeded the French in Indochina with a determination to stop the communist march. This is a curious morality, assisting all sides in a conflict when the conflict has nothing whatever to do with you. In fact, Vietnam exposed the fundamental immorality of American foreign policy. The popular logic of the sixties held that the US had to lose the war if she was to be morally good.

America could fight in Vietnam without reserves only because of the Baby Boom. And there were enough left over to point out that what America was doing made no sense, even in the most rhapsodic American context. Of 58,220 casualties of this "wrong analysis," a quarter weren't given the choice but had been drafted.

Attrition entered the battle lexicon through understanding losses as something other than lives of young Americans. In such a habit of mind, attrition takes on a psychological as well as a physical dimension. The mind then acquires a new habit that in the last century has leaned ponderously on race.

Periodically, habits might be shaken and upended. Much of Western ethics traces to the ancient fables of Aesop, simply Greek for "Ethiopian." Through his changing identity, Malcolm Little ("Malcolm X," then "el-Hajj Malik el-Shabazz") concluded that any black movement confined to America was doomed. The problem is one not of civil rights, and therefore domestic—but of human rights and therefore global.

The black American's legacy is a struggle of two souls and the Third World. Think of the disproportionate number of black soldiers who have fallen in all of America's conflicts, then double it. It would profit everyone to reconsider the implications of Dr. Leaky's remarkable find and just what is owed the souls of each other.

CHAPTER NINE

Waiting for Change

Everywhere I go, I'm asked if I think the universities stifle writers. My opinion is that they don't stifle enough of them.
— Flannery O'Connor

SOMEONE HAS SAID YOU can tell a good deal about the character and habits of a country by watching its waiters. It's impossible to name a country where there are none, though at any given moment yours may be nowhere to be seen. True, many and various persons are called to wait, and there undeniably are differences in how a single waiter may perform from time to time. He may seem to prefer certain patrons to others. By and large, however, there are revealing national tendencies that may be observed.

Solemn professionalism, for example—the *métier* of the French waiter—has been mistaken for arrogance. He is only manifesting his skill to raise your enjoyment to a standard far beyond what you could imagine or desire. By contrast, Hungarian waiters work in pairs, to assure adequate service and provide the constant threat of music at the table. In Italy, you can always press the waiter for his candid recommendation, which he will offer by pulling up a chair and joining your party to be certain everyone hears his suggestion and complicated rationale. It is getting harder to find an English waiter in London. When he does appear, he is either the obsequious sort who thanks you with every service he performs, or the kind that accepts your declared wishes as if you had just given him the correct answer to the *Times* crossword. He then thanks you smartly for your help.

At length, one comes to the American waiter, who embodies a paradox. It is an American enigma of one independent, self-reliant adult performing personal and rudimentary services for another, equally capable adult who allows him or herself to be served. Equality, in fact, is at the heart of it for those who take the part of the American waiter. It is accepting one role today with full knowledge that roles may be exchanged, duties and stations reversed, perhaps as soon as breakfast tomorrow.

Self-reliance is deeply burrowed into the American mind. There is confidence in a capacity for individual regeneration, and no limits have yet been reached for the American traits of sagacity or silliness, magnificence or miscalculation. Immutable self-reliance vests this fluid process of regeneration. For more than a hundred years, regenerative capacity has led to inventing the self over and over again. Donning the professional habit, the spirit is pulled through the sleeve and somehow dresses the self, anew. This is the great testament of self-reliance. But dependence upon the pragmatic self simply leads to mourning that vanishing side—recalled as the genuine, authentic, erudite self—well-prepared and cerebrally balanced.

One curious consequence of missing the erudite self is substituting over-education. It has spawned another phenomenon entirely, called by some the arrogance of credentialing. This creates problems. For on the one hand, gaining credentials supports individual achievement, but on the other, it erodes the virtue of self-reliance through the emptiness of hierarchy and fatuous security of a certificate. What's worse, in a sufficiently robust economy, the confused over-credentialed professional may well be delivered into an imaginary state of grace.

The stubborn proof of this is all around. During the early eighties, a prosperous New England community faced yet another labor strike by their school bus drivers, whose permanent addresses often were not known, let alone their credentials. Rather than give the striking scoundrels any satisfaction, a dozen reproving mothers took over the duties, driving their children to and from school for the remaining term of the labor contract. The town newspaper observed that it was the first time every bus had a driver who held at least one master's degree.

One or two of these mothers no doubt had waited tables in graduate school. Far from immune to this condition, women have also been drawn to American educational wanderlust. By 1985, the number of doctoral degrees conferred upon women at US universities exceeded that for men. Pursuit of a doctorate at that time had involved about ten years, on average—ten years of income foregone, self-reliance delayed.

Advanced degrees in the physical sciences have consistently taken the least time to achieve, and perhaps not surprisingly, education doctorates take the most time. Explanations for this have diverged. Some authorities feel physical scientists are more easily satisfied, or more disciplined and trusting—and less imaginative, overall. This may be evidence that it is easier to learn than to teach, and hardest of all is preparing another to teach, with or without them having learned. Possessed of a remarkable facility for learning and little interest in teaching, philosopher Immanuel Kant is reported to have characterized the academic lecture as that process by which the notes of the instructor are transposed into the notes of the student without passing through the mind of either.

Since long before Theodore Roosevelt beat the idea to death, there has been a national article of faith that history is not kind to idlers. Schooling may be unreflective and bereft of thinking, but it is based on the idea of keeping busy. Education these days is not so much a matter of preserving our scientific and cultural inheritance as it is honing skills that will make for a productive time in industry. Many a student has been nurtured by soft, collective capitalist consciousness.

The truly learned muse as to whether the shared sense of value naturally occurs as an active or a passive state. They see little hope of redemption for the somnolent student who interrupts to ask the teacher whether Richard III personally resented Shakespeare's portrayal of him. Today, everyone has an equal opportunity to neglect his or her education.

By the same token, most have known persons who fully realize themselves as a reference work. These few look to increase mental weight by adding factual calories. They demonstrate intellect through a multitude of connections that appear obscure to everyone else. The word *Yggdrasill*, for example, seems a curious and shadowy, ancient thing. Yet those who took the right courses quickly see the contemporary relevance of the "world tree," the great ash with its roots in the underworld, the axis on which the heavens pivot.

Etymology is an especially good example of a more general failing—namely, the endless pursuit of factual trifles for purposes of intellectual intimidation. The chief by-product of schooling in the Middle Ages, this form of scholastic tyranny offers both entertainment and fulfillment.

To follow a word that has blossomed in English back to its seedpod in the germinating ancestral vernacular is to unearth an easy addiction. Words on loan arrive on the wind from all directions. Take, for example, *tempo* (Italian) and *tempura* (Japanese). The Latin *tempus*, meaning time, has the plural *tempora* and is the progenitor of the Italian for time, tempo, which in turn wafted into the English language as a musical term. When the Portuguese became the first Europeans to visit Japan, it was noticed that they would substitute seafood for meat during Lent (in Latin, *tempora quadragesima*, "the times of the forty"). Completely neglecting the obscurity of the catechism, the Japanese eventually saw that *tempura* referred to fried seafood.

These misadventures are so remote and time-consuming that it's hard to stop. *Mahatma* comes from the Hindi and "atmosphere" from Greek roots. The Indo-European root *at-men* has the meaning "breath" and is seen in German *atmen* as "breathe," Sanskrit *atman* as "soul" and the Greek *atmos* as "smoke" or "vapor." *Maha-atma* is contracted in Hindi to *mahatma*, meaning "great soul." "Atmosphere" thus became the enveloping space that holds all essences, the "air-sphere."

It turns out that the antidote for this debilitating affliction is also provided by institutional education. The cure is *empirical subject matter*. By applying mnemonic devices to the body of scientific knowledge one may vanquish an otherwise enfeebling obsession. The commendable result can be the crisp recall of all twelve cranial nerves, remembering the first twenty digits in the decimal expansion of π, or reciting the astronomical designations given to the spectral types of the main sequence of stars.

Diversity in how to become self-reliant ensures that the bottom of the well of impractical education can never be plumbed. It is part of an ancient inheritance and an all-around worthy thing. Even so, it is helpful to have the occasional reminder that anything that can be taught by one to another is relatively inconsequential. The prize of self-discovery is not won without effort. Bedeviled by the state of evaporative education, the merciful end is the award of a degree, which gives no benefit to those few who thought they had pursued something else. This suggests it would be better to do away with teaching and training if what the student really is after is thinking and learning.

Yet education persists. Imagine a *Parable of Forty*, having nothing to do with Lent and Japanese seafood but illustrating how far education has come in two or three millennia. Forty was once the life expectancy for a healthy human who was able to avoid war and other hazards. Life spans have been extended dramatically, despite continued conflict and many an unusual entree served by the wait staff. In developed economies, forty is now often the age at which one's education either is finished (not to imply complete) or otherwise deferred.

Lawyers are everyone's favorite object lesson. The United States has four percent of the world's population, 18 percent of its economy, 22 percent of its prisoners, and 70 percent of its lawyers. The fundamental precept of the *rule of law* is taken seriously, and it is clear just how much help is needed with it. As it happens, in general, lawyers make good waiters, and the latter-day rise of the lawyer legions has created large numbers of well-schooled lawyers-in-waiting.

Our *Parable of Forty* also implies that humans have old and new brains—one part that preserves primitive divisions and differential integrity, and a new part needed for adaptation and change. Many a PhD candidate will insist there is successive accretion and specialization of those old structures sitting atop the spinal cord, with new functions being added all the time. Writing and reading as new functional abilities brought on increased self-reliance. The ability to gain experience and to learn the basics of an art or science from a written memory without having to rely on a benevolent master was a spectacular advance.

The connection of education to the meaning of self-reliance is that one is self-made. The first really American advice on how to sort things out came from New Yorker Walt Whitman. His view of the country, from under the Brooklyn Bridge, was a mingling of commerce, art, and science bathed in soft gaslight. He approached life as something to be made from the unmade. Whitman thought the beauty of humanity was easily seen in America's boldness and simplicity.

Self-making was part of the memory of the species, and it is wise to follow it—even while making it all up. While a curious national ambivalence has put a Walt Whitman High School in many a state in the Union there's not a local school board anywhere that would be comfortable if Walt were found teaching in one of them.

In self-making, future experiences are shaped by expressions of recent experiences. Either chances for repeating the same experience over and over improve, or the wrong thing is expressed the first time around and future chances for the experience are missed. The Pentateuch tells us that humankind was evicted from Paradise and forced to leave Eden for the workplace. Toil was laid upon the human spirit, which might otherwise have been left to soar in weightless grace. The Benedictines took the position, without saying so out loud, that "to work is to pray." But some confess they have made it their business to avoid both whenever possible.

Part of the residue of self-making is that careers have been replaced by individualized expressions of both the bane of toil and the practical necessity of work. A common contemporary interpretation of the term "career" is a succession of positions, which demands continual public marketing of the self-made self. The personal literature that results from this circus of intention has been good for lawyers. It takes someone who is obdurate about his or her protracted education to handle the details.

The multi-talented-over-educated are witness to the disquiet of unpredictable change. In recent years, well-trained scholars of empty fluencies are being laid off in large numbers while blue collar skills are in steady demand at the same time prestigious universities are reverting to their traditional role of helping us see that self-reliance has little to do with job training. Things one needs to know beyond trades have a value that rests within. Anyone can feel he or she is living according to the *law of natural rejection*.

The prototype for American creative subjectivity is Walt Whitman's *Song of Myself*, with its stylistic blend of miscellany and Biblical parallel. Most enduring is Whitman's method of creating the self in an extension of the moment through a metaphor of musical abstraction. Once compared to T.S. Eliot's *The Waste Land*, *Song of Myself* haunts readers in the same way; its meaning seems to slide out of reach. What is left are themes of the open road, the doorway, the crossing. Whitman was imagining for everybody else. He kept returning to essential things, remaking himself each time, shaping and re-shaping his vast poem, which was unlike anything in the previous century. His erotic images were taken from astronomy, massacre, solitary women, sunsets, sadness, and prayer. The poem told no story. It made no argument. The *song* pulls itself out of time even as it takes all of time and the universe as its melody. The song is about *self*.

Emerson knew the poet as "Walt" rather than Walter Whitman Jr., just as he himself, as a young man, had chosen to be known as "Waldo" to avoid the less appealing "Ralph." David Henry Thoreau became "Henry David" in the same sort of shuffled identity. None of these names is quite the same as it once was. Each has remade itself. In the end, the multi-talented must be proficient at blending comedy and modernity.

Working has made Americans lean heavily on the end of the week but uniqueness is to be found in the uncommon ability to regenerate periodically in a singular and original relation to the universe. One is capable of rising above blindness, truculence, and waste by pretending to be better than she or he probably is. Then she pulls herself through the sleeve.

Belief in possibility is the habit that distinguishes Americans from European cultural cousins. It makes the image of Walt Whitman as waiter at T.S. Eliot's table a completely satisfying picture. It is that quality that allows each to take the part of the singing waiter from time to time between periods of employment.

CHAPTER TEN

Hymn to Hypatia

Gertrude was always right.
— Ernest Hemingway

For many centuries, women were barred from taking part in the musical aspects of religious ceremony and ritual, officially excluded from the performance of art composed for the liturgy. Shut off from this spiritual grace, women had even less to say about the sublime practice of creating music. There are no satisfying explanations for how this alleged spiritual and musical inferiority came to be. No one can say why this attitude persisted. Yet more than one renowned conductor has insisted *women ruin music*, as these maestros fiddle and quaver with rationales for why this is so.

In the medieval university curriculum, men were schooled in music as part of the *quadrivium*, which also included arithmetic, geometry, and astronomy—or simply, the "language of science." For a long time, the ludicrous justification cited for conspicuous lack of achievement by women in, for example, the "mathematical arts" was a natural and enduring inferiority—*women must have no aptitude for higher things*. In science, philosophy, numberless disciplines, and countless professions women historically have been given less encouragement and correspondingly reduced access to the masters.

Curiously, Americans now are more aware that persons, communities, individual potential, and private aspirations are very often defined through gender. But it's not understood all that well. Many insist that in one way or another, institutions and popular conventions continue to neglect, discourage, and destroy smart women in a gender-duet of self-deception and mutual confusion.

One day during the Lenten season in the year 415 CE, a chariot turned the corner in a crowded street of the Egyptian city of Alexandria. It carried to lectures a distinguished mathematician, astronomer, and philosopher. The culmination of this short ride has been described as the passing of an epoch, the end of the age of Greek reasoning, dialectic, and spiritual culture and the emergence of dogma and excess in the form of Christian civil hierarchies. Passing along with reason was the common, though spectacular, achievement of women. In earlier times, women had been every bit the equal of men, given free expression, and considered to possess both divine intelligence and natural beauty—mystically bound to laws of the universe. These attributes were combined in woman and made her superior to man. In her chariot stood Hypatia.

Virtuous Hypatia was dazzling in the bloom of her beauty. There was a loftiness of her wisdom and humility in her modest manner. Many young students attended her lectures. In literary mythologies, Hypatia emerges as the spirit of Plato and the body of Aphrodite—a transcendent figure of

Hellenism. She allowed herself to be noticed in public places, showing little restraint in her behavior and liberal license in her speech.

Apart from the rich legends surrounding her receding lifetime, it is reliably claimed that by the age of twenty-five, Hypatia was well known as an accomplished algebraist, curator of the great library at Alexandria, and interpreter of the Platonic view of being. Her passing not only ended the flower of Greek thought but signaled the stirrings that would become the Christian Dark Ages.

The Philosopher of Alexandria stood on the shoulders of her impressive cultural and spiritual forebears: Sappho, poet of the Aegean and lyricist of ancient Greece; Aspasia of Miletus; Cleopatra; Boudica, warrior regent of the Iceni of Britain. Through Hypatia's legacy we can imagine the beginnings of how men and women differentially came to see themselves. Hypatia stands as a moment of antiquity that points toward our time.

Women who *do* are anomalies and mad creatures. So history has gone. Obliterated women, starved and battered out of consciousness, return in unexpected places. Like mythic Ariadne, women unable themselves to escape, lead men through the labyrinth. Women who have called themselves *George* and worse have authored unconventional lives, capturing the limited imagination of a large and raucous audience of self-anointed male authorities.

License to *do* is generally granted by the community. It takes the form of *who is permitted to do what*. The community at large has assumed this leads to everything being done better. Assent as to how things should be done has created many nagging problems. There appears to be a built-in ethical clause regulating society that allows for exceptions. Any person with a remarkable endowment of intellect can grant himself license to *do*. Men have defined just how *intelligence* is to be spotted so all can know when, where, and exactly for whom exceptions are to be made. Men have agreed intelligence is the faculty that allows one to undertake the difficult, the complex, and the abstract. Finally, it is all done according to some social value, that is, it's worth doing, and something original emerges. One view surviving in the twentieth-century held that manifest expressions of intelligence are more often evident in men. Elsewhere, intelligence was considered rare. It did not normally migrate to non-males.

Disruptive women—that is, women who *did* things, were explained as peculiar, functioning outside their natural domain. Earlier, the popular term coined for disorganized thinking in females, leading to this observable condition of peculiarity was "hysteria." Oddly enough, no one has yet found histologic evidence of somatic changes present in the hysterical subject—nothing to suggest a clinical diagnosis except obvious psychic derangement.

Ancient physicians, however, were able not only to determine the cause but to explain why this was observed pretty much exclusively in women. Until about two hundred years ago, the explanation sounded right to modern physicians too. They decided hysteria was caused by disturbances of the uterus (in Greek, *hysteros*). Female behavior could become morbid due to the wandering of the organ that, according to what was known about it, was supposed to "lag behind"—the actual root meaning of the name.

Medical science has since recognized its error. But socially, even therapeutically, the ancient concept and specious explanation remain useful to some men. The hysterical subject is described as incapable of taking in fields of consciousness in customary ways. She acts on the impulse of the moment, she is open to external suggestion, she gives undue weight to emotions—to transient states of awareness and to memory. There is ample evidence that symptoms of this female pathology have been repeatedly mistaken in the male for genius, for originality on the rise. Can anyone really take this sort of fanciful proposition seriously? Imagine such a distorted view reading something like this:

> *Hysteria is more common among Latin than Teutonic peoples. Rarely seen in England, it is rampant in much of France. Our understanding of this is rooted in extreme emotionalism: a constant craving for sympathy and an irrational desire for universal acceptance. Drugs have not helped. The cure is moral treatment and it is crucial, for the wandering hysteros may ramble into insanity.*

Some writers of the sisterhood beg the question and seize upon the notion of *smart women* to make it an anthem. No doubt this emboldens women and gives everyone hope. But this may not help either. Smart women presumably are in contradistinction to *women*. This begins to sound like our familiar confusion.

An immutable debt is owed to smart women. They are the ones who make themselves known to others first as mind and heart. Characteristics of gender may follow at some point but do not precede the mind. They are something besides women, able to suspend disbelief and master silly rituals of induction into commercial or academic or scientific circles without actually endorsing the partisan process. They are women and something else, in the way a smart doctor is skilled at the healing arts, plays Debussy on the piano, and is successful with her investments.

First order intelligence, when joined to female power, is more essence in a single being than many men can bear. Men may feel it is only fair to pare down some of this mystic energy so as to make woman mortal. Once more, there is the question of whose standards of logic are to be used and why should women be forced continually to lower theirs? It is a desperate and meaningless syllogism for men to declare that *all* women are smart. Instead men simply could begin to believe that all women are women. This should be enough.

One story carried away from Hypatia's school may include rare fragments containing some of her own words. She took pains to teach that wisdom commands we search for the mysterious and the indefinite—that when we reach the far fringes of knowledge, beyond the body, there we find understanding. Beauty is in the self and above bodily perfection.

At one point, a young student fell in love with Hypatia and with utter lack of control (though not hysteria, probably) he confessed to her his passionate feelings. She of ethical fortitude resolved to lead the young man to understanding and, at the same time, chase him off. Hypatia is said to have shown him her article of intimate feminine hygiene and remonstrated about his misapprehension of the physical aspect. She told him the worldly body was what he loved and not beauty for its own sake.

Well, the only way for many to believe Hypatia capable of such a spectacle is to see this as in keeping with the true character of the woman, according to how her legend has survived. Repugnant and unwholesome, this vignette is, in fact, wholly Platonic. Wise Hypatia, endowed with an attractive form, set her pleasing, sympathetic mind against the concrete and visible qualities of the sensible world. She taught that the intellect delights in pure things and needs to hurry away from shadows and clouded images and traces of beauty man believes he has found in physical bodies.

Gender equality has had the effect of demoting the male, as he sees it, making it relatively more difficult for him to realize his potential. Women start out as girls, and we continue to learn about ways Nature favors females. Girls talk earlier than do boys, develop stronger vocabularies sooner, learn to read earlier, and excel in language and logical (rather than rote) memory. It's been suggested that some men may feel the need to make things ever more abstract, to be certain they maintain the advantage in "intelligence." "She was a curious equation," one man wrote, "who attracted many a mathematician."

There seems to be an established natural superiority of women that may be present *in utero* where, medical men might remind us, each of us starts out life as female. The greatest part of intellectual development has to do with environment; if young women were to receive equal favor and like opportunity, the age-old myths of female intellectual inferiority that linger in the remote villages and corporate boardrooms would no doubt vanish in a generation. If anyone is competitively disadvantaged in connection with human practices of *doing*, it is not women.

One professor of comparative mythology suggested the female governs time according to herself. A complete and timeless world exists in every woman. Man, by contrast, is profoundly guilty of only being present to things, and this, only from time to time. It is a mistaken aphorism to say a man is *living in a world of his own*. He's lucky to find a woman who will let him into any world. It's futile to try to imagine man having the genetic skills to create a world. Women, in turn, may fail to remember that men are only men—nothing more. They have real and profound limitations. For their part, men mistakenly believe this somehow is an excuse.

Before the advent of psychology, American women were looking out from behind the curtain of marriage and writing about the female self—intoxications only women can know. References came out of experiences of women living alone, or in close proximity to other women, or in "Boston marriages," a New England term in centuries past to describe two women living together independent of financial support from a man. So often fit for higher forms of art, politics, and science, many women have been brilliant in the ways they have qualified themselves to do less.

More than a century ago, American novelist Kate Chopin offered incisive commentary on prevailing social attitudes and struggles of women. *The Awakening*, published in 1899, now is seen as a work of psychological complexity and among the earliest explorations of feminism. It has been described as anticipating writing of Faulkner and Hemingway on topics of gender roles, social constraints, romanticism and solitude.

Men are permitted to know more of women when women feel either secure or irresponsible enough to help them understand. Control over moral and reproductive destiny has made all the difference for the last few generations. With the car, the pill, and the vote have come a ringing and welcome voice for women—first, among themselves, then slowly to the others who will never be women, or most probably never will be.

As each woman is of her own world and making, the end of every woman is her own private suicide, floating out with the tides, rivulets of ebbing awareness against her naked beauty. Learned woman is educated to support and guide a species she herself has created. She longs to know that she is becoming something. Often a woman chooses the means of her own destruction; in Kate Chopin's phrase, "…making such a mess of things and working out her own damnation." Smart women would like to have had things go differently.

As her chariot slowed before a noisy crowd, Hypatia looked on the throng of angry faces. Gibbon wrote that "rumors had circulated that named Hypatia as the obstacle to reconciliation of the pagan and Christian, the male and the female." Her personal beliefs and strange facility with unfeminine disciplines of mathematics and philosophy amounted to witchcraft that offended just about everybody in the street. That fatal day, she was torn from her chariot, stripped naked, and dragged to a church called the Caesareum. There, Hypatia was murdered, her flesh lacerated with oyster shells, "her quivering limbs delivered to the flames."

Abominations immediately force us to take sides. Portraits of Hypatia have been sketched over and over, but the view alleging her many heresies against the Church did not last. Christianity delivered itself. Literary sympathizers declared her a martyr, even a confessor, while the Church effected her conversion to the Faith. A bit of her story is known today in reading the life of Saint Catherine. Hypatia's divinity is as indescribable as the silent ecstasies of a woman's life cast anew. Her gentle arms rest on pillars through which all may pass from the twenty-first century into the fifth, and back again.

One day in the last few years of the second millennium CE, two thousand kilometers north of the ruins of the Caesareum, a hundred men voted to name a woman, the first woman, a permanent member of the Vienna Philharmonic Orchestra.

3

BOOK OF VOYAGES

Revisiting decades of the seventies and eighties…

Voyages toward full upright adulthood meant finding a place by leaving it.

The middle of Europe is Roman, Greek and Slav, described as being full of movement, not knowing where it is moving.

There is danger in being both bold and weak, and many await the vandals' return.

Empire runs its course, and reordering doctrine eventually goes the way of empire, as villages revive their myths.

Intellectual breeding grounds of liberty include monuments to some vision of the future and the notion of social equality.

CHAPTER ELEVEN

Kansas Valkyrie

Draw in your head and sleep the long way home.
— Hart Crane

Postal errors account for a number of American place names. Having the sense of a place and labeling it is so important that once a name is settled, there is great reluctance to change it. Sometimes names do get changed for a while to see how everyone likes it. Usually, enough don't very much, and names revert, reappear, or simply rectify a temporary confusion. For real change, someone must subvert, misspell or corrupt a name until others become comfortable with it. By now, generations in the canyons along the river have grown comfortable with the western American slang for it, "Picketwire." Most probably, you are ready to guess at the frontier origins of the name. It likely comes from fencing used long ago to tame the land into parcels. Naming a place indeed closes it in and identifies it for everyone, so they can find the way back after having left it for some other place. A name protects a place from accident.

Before the mail started arriving regularly, the town had the name the French trappers had given it, *Purgatoire*. Most of the French soon left, and through poor diction, bad spelling and divine providence, French was displaced by North American Anglo-Saxon. Spelling limbo has created a postal purgatory for everybody.

Looking for bigger places beyond right here sometimes turns out to be simply searching for bigger thoughts. One clear example is Thomas More's *Utopia*, which set a certain tone with his fictional view of an island that is to be found "Nowhere." Whether it was supposed to be Polynesia or Peru, Utopia was the modern, sixteenth-century version of an ancient notion, meant to describe what European states could become, if based only on reason. Much of the atmosphere of the story is reported to have been lifted from the narrative of the travels of Amerigo Vespucci and the *Cosmographiæ*. Europe had a persistent hope that bigger thoughts of almost unimaginable places lay on a course to the West, the New World.

It was the Dutch who named "America." Stay-at-home geographer Martin Waldseemüller mistakenly accredited the discovery of the New World to Amerigo Vespucci, merchant, adventurer, and by several accounts, shrewd opportunist. Martin nominated the name "America" in April of 1507, seeing no possible objection, "since both Europe and Asia took their names from women."

From the Middle Ages on, Western knowledge has tended to move still further westward from the east. In the East, Persians enjoyed their intellectual rebirth as keepers of the ancient Greek texts for that extended period during which the Greeks misplaced their wisdom. Amid the ruins of Ctesiphon, Persian scholars succeeded in introducing secular humanism before the West had a chance to name it.

The New World looked to the Orient (literally, "below the horizon") and imagined places where thoughts are so big that they fill all available space, piling up on one another through history so as to get a clear view of Nowhere.

In a similar vein, turn-of-the-century American fabulist Lyman Frank Baum begins the story of a journey from Kansas to see the crowned heads of Europe but a storm pulls toward utopian Oz. Drawn off the plains, the road now leads to the crowded glimmering streets and vertical thoughts of the Emerald City. Trapped in a journey that ever increases the distance from home, this keeps up until thoughts become big enough to recoil and sling back to the familiar.

Leaving the sweet plains, many Americans, aimless and filled with good intentions, were carried on silvery zephyrs to the lands of Giotto, Monet, Paderewski, and those primal sources of otherworldly imaginings—the monasteries and the Brothers Grimm. The only way back home was forward to a place unknown, and many were ready to take advice from any munchkin.

For many, Europe was the means for revealing American qualities. Some learned the romantic coinage of the banjo and the buffalo, bartering American frontier loot for nudes, philosophies, and table wine. To learn about America, a growing company found they had to leave it. A fair number sought to witness the ancient and sublime. A splendid Oz it surely was for many a wandering Dorothy.

Here was a new place, the Olde World. Young frauds aspired to put off compromise for as long as possible and go to Europe for a look. Better yet, study in Europe (study anything in Europe) to be grounded in all vicarious subjects: architecture, idealism, immortality.

The stolid daughter of affluence and indolent son of permissiveness set themselves adrift in venerable neighborhoods.

Ideals are kept alive in stories secular missionaries retell. Close to three thousand years back, Homer was codifying all the stories. His Odysseus is the hero of the West—bored, reluctant, undisciplined—but cunning, capable, and virtuous. According to the rule of *someone even more so lives to the east*, Odysseus may well have heard the tale of antiquity's great hero Gilgamesh, who must have been even less disciplined.

Most everyone's attention is easily drawn to Odysseus and his journey. As the epic begins, everyone else is home or has died trying to get there. With the wisdom of Athene, his own courage and heart, Odysseus endures dangers and humiliations. He has been hidden from everyone, save the gods, by Calypso (Secret) for seven years following the Trojan War.

Odysseus's one hope remains to return home to Ithaca, where Penelope is trying her best to stay in charge of things. All his tests and trials are irrational to this reluctant adventurer, yet he must persevere in order to return. Odysseus is the counterbalance for Homer. Achilles was all anger and grief. Odysseus is that human desire to snatch happiness from disaster.

This was such a good story that Plato recast it. In his own version, Socrates willingly leaves his place, the city named for wise Athene, to investigate the Good. Ontology of the *Republic* is based on the individual as the reservoir for aspects of the Good, among them, intelligence, courage, and something else that combines reason, spirit and desire. He calls this *justice*.

From his chair in Chicago much later on, L. Frank Baum surmised that folklore, myths, legends, and fairy tales were timeless. He recognized Homer as a fine resource for teaching morality. In 1900, however, Baum reportedly felt that morality was covered sufficiently in modern education, so the sole purpose of his story, *The Wonderful Wizard of Oz*, was to entertain. He wanted to recall to mind the childhood joy of life, without nightmare, misery, or horror.

He may have been too modest. Dorothy's quest with her companions—the dull-witted, the scared, the numb—is a fair American retelling of Homer and Plato, all wrapped up in Art Deco. The traveler is delivered out of irrationality, complete. From the ineffable salons of the Emerald City, she is sent whirling, and in an instant she is sitting on the broad Kansas plain. So capricious is the weather in the Midwest.

The perpetual notion of human permanence is immortality. This is an abstraction foreign to the children of the children of L. Frank Baum. A European cast of mind, immortality is not necessarily attractive in America. In the dim mists of Euro-history, the *waelcyraei* hovered above in the service of the Norse god Odin, pointing out warriors worthy of immortality—that is, heroes who would die in battle and be spirited to Paradise. Literally "choosers of the slain," Valkyrie were fully-armored women who had complete dominion over men. They conducted the valiant and the pure of heart to a particular place, guarding things, as Penelope had done, until some presumed ultimate judgment when they would see whether the Valkyrie had made the right choices. Americans kibitz on the idea of immortality and find it vicariously exciting. No one here really wants a ticket.

Why immortality, Americans may ask, and what's the point anyhow? One answer may explain why millions of young souls climbed into the balloon to Europe. There is something in the world that is serious, and somehow humans overlap it. Valkyrie ease the way for the chosen. Going back to Europe became a young person's act of witness.

Scouring the Continent, dizzy mortals looked for something the Olde World could contribute to the New. This American tradition had been well established. Jefferson had been there in the nascent days of the intellectual revolution in France, but he had come more for the wine and society. Franklin similarly had come to accept exuberant adoration by the French.

As it had been for Jefferson and Franklin in their time, the early seventies were an excellent point to leave behind familiar places for personal adventure. Rediscovered was the conscience of the tripper and the perennial train passenger. Everywhere was a fresh view of home, like the prospect enjoyed by those hovering armored women. Yet is it ever where you think it should be?

Bearings are easily lost in traveling. John Philip Sousa is a symbol of exuberance and is thought by all to be the American anthem made flesh. It turns out he studied with Offenbach and played viola, or some other military band instrument, in Offenbach's orchestra in Paris. He came to write marches in the French style—that is, he copied the popular French quick tempo of 120 beats-per-minute. America adopted his marches, wedding patriotism to the military (a common failing of many nations), and it was suddenly easier to see why Americans walk fast, "like the French." *It must be that American Sousa's national marches!* Sousa had a Prussian mother; his father was Portuguese.

Europe has long been a curiosity to Americans, a true Oz of a place. Kansas bears eponymous inscriptions of foreign places and past times. Topeka is the Kaw Indian designation of "the place to find small potatoes." The prairie town, to which someone returned after seeing Paris, is called *Bel Pre*. We have Kismet, Kansas in a nod to a Turkish Odin. There are Zenda, Kansas and Ulysses, Kansas. Elsmore, Kansas probably was how the post office came to spell "Elsinore." L. Frank Baum recognized something lasting here. He was, after all, a contemporary of both Mark Twain and Cornelius Vanderbilt, each a wry observer of the special contradictions that made the American soufflé rise.

Naturally skeptical of anything as enduring as immortality, Americans have difficulty taking it seriously, reminding brothers and sisters to *"pay no attention to that man behind the curtain!"*

The film version of *The Wizard of Oz*, up against *Stagecoach*, *Wuthering Heights* and *Gone with the Wind*, won nothing at the twelfth Academy Awards of 1939. It remains pure and uncorrupted as our own classical exegesis of the universal journey to places with odd names.

CHAPTER TWELVE

Tempo di Valse

All great art is born of the metropolis.
— Ezra Pound

LIFE LEAVES SO MUCH out. It's as if one is sitting on the verandah, in the twilight of everyday, waiting to be invited into the *living room*. Instead, he only hears the sounds from inside. This he takes as proof, both that there is an inexpressible, crystalline world he desires to inhabit and that he has been left out of it. Music escapes and drifts outside to tell the essential truth of life. Skeptics may admit that music helps move things along with spirited cheer, quickly enough so as not to pause and over-examine one's limitations, yet not too fast. Musical thoughts, waves of sound coming off the score, were Wittgenstein's great clue to how language holds the world still so that he could understand it. He used to sit on his verandah, listening to his gramophone, in his geometrical house, in Parkgasse, in Vienna.

Vienna. There was a time when Vienna was for many young Americans traveling in Europe the model for so much of what life should not leave out. *Die Stadt* exists under a halo of the improbable, generated by its own balance, distrusting both underplaying and overdoing. It makes the rules.

The secret charm of all this is *fortwursteln*, or, for the English, "muddling through." Americans lack it; the rest of the world is out of stock as well. Just as Europe was rediscovering South America and the Far East, Austrian Robert Musil was writing *Der Mann ohne Eigenschaften*. Though never completed, *The Man Without Qualities* offers a modern metaphor for the struggle to stay in touch with the human spirit in the face of cataclysmic world change. As a center of gravity, Vienna heroically holds onto itself for a little longer than the rest. It is a modern city, but it will not move too fast, filled with zest but in a free cadence to be savored. It maintains its pace.

The American visitor still hears that Vienna is a dream city and is prepared to believe it's true. Vienna seems to have its own idea of nature and of life's essential ingredients; it fills the senses—it is the home of the psychological but accommodates the mystical. For the Viennese, it is a dream city for practical reasons. Like Venice, it imagined itself and dreamed the place into consciousness. Life here is grounded in the language, the grammar of dreams. Its inhabitants have maintained some safe distance from the main thoroughfares of success.

The City is an old abstraction that beckons to youth. Its outward and visible symbol is opera. Its opera is *Der Rosenkavalier*. Nothing else shows Vienna so well, filled as it is with anachronism, all miraculous anodynes, thoroughly unhistorical but somehow plausible. From the music of Strauss and text of Hofmannsthal, the audience is given a glimpse of what lies beyond Romanticism. Life needs fast-moving conversation, heightened by music. Brilliant Vienna is from a time before long ago.

Museums around the City show the unique Viennese perspective formed at the crossroads of Europe, the intersection of three great European civilizations: Roman, German, Slav. Two thousand years ago, Vienna was a Roman camp in good wine country called *vindobona*. Armies of the Crusades tracked through about the time Walther von der Vogelweide, great *Minnesänger* of the Viennese court, was helping shape the Nibelung sagas into an epic poem. Then at the end of the thirteenth century, the house of Hapsburg arrived.

The Hapsburgs liked conquest, also marriage. Indeed, marriage was the battlefield that brought them Burgundy, Flanders, Castile, Bohemia, and Hungary, and set up joint ventures on several other thrones farther from home. Austria became Europe's bastion against the constant incursions of the Turks, who thought Vienna a mythical empire and a great prize. Besieged but never yielding, Vienna finally pushed the Turkish menace back into the Balkans toward the end of the seventeenth century. So enormous was Vienna's relief that this event inaugurated the most dazzling era of Austrian culture.

There was the effect Suleiman the Magnificent and Vizier Kara Mustafa had on everyone. Viennese called this highly ornate and extravagant style "the Baroque." The City that was the diametrical opposite of what steppe nomad and weary marauder had dreamed of became an improbable cultural fantasy of monasteries and palaces.

Guide books are no help in Vienna. There is nothing like Hilaire Belloc's *Paris* or Hans Christian Andersen's

Lisbon—no advice on how to set the experience at hand. Vienna is not, strictly speaking, a destination but always on the way to somewhere else. It lies on the path to some other destination. Vienna occurs during the rapid-eye-movement portion of the journey. For the forty-five years of the Austro-Hungarian Dual Monarchy, Vienna gathered in many races and component nations of the Empire.

The whole reason for Vienna is fun. There are majestic structures and twinkling corners of celebration. Huge closed gondolas of its Riesenrad Ferris wheel are devoted to amusement and dedicated to diversion. The Hofburg is the center of Vienna, and actually another city itself with twenty-six hundred rooms in the palace. Another fifteen hundred rooms have been set aside exclusively for fun at the summer palace, Schönbrunn. Up the hill and beyond the Gloriette arch lies the solitude of elysian fields and a view of the rooftops of Vienna. At dusk, their pink, blue, and orange flames shimmer on the Danube.

Vienna's Innenstadt is populated by bronze likenesses of many musicians, a dozen writers, several artists, and a handful of Social Democrats. As a meeting place for the pantheon of eighteenth and nineteenth century composers, Vienna introduced Beethoven to Haydn. Both remain. Beethoven's bronze colossus sits just off the Schubert-Ring. Life left much out for Schubert, but for this brief thirty-one years and the noble ideas he put into sound, Franz Schubert sits at the edge of the blue-green enchantment of the immense *Stadtpark*. Between Beethoven and Schubert stands the progenitor of Vienna's own musical dreams, Johann Strauss, fiddle in hand. His dizzying array of elegant notions flowed out as the *waltz*.

Vienna is animated by the waltz. There have been many periods when the waltz alone kept away the embalmer's fluid. Americans are told a story that Old Man Strauss, wary of the devastating virus of the waltz, sought to immunize his sons. He insisted Johann II train for that species of dependable cynicism, investment banking, and Josef was to be an architect. Eduard, the youngest, he gave not to the Church but to the law. Johann Strauss died in the afternoon of September 25, 1849. On September 26 all three sons were writing waltzes.

The modern City of Vienna sustains in a comfortable rhythm, *tempo di valse* (Italian, meaning "time spent"). What makes Vienna modern to the American sensibility is mostly the art nouveau aesthetic of architect Otto Wagner. He and a band of comrades formed the Secession, a union of plastic and graphic geniuses prepared to force innovation down the throats of Austria and all Europe. Their oft-repeated motto read, "To the Age Its Art, to Art Its Freedom."

Painter Gustav Klimt was the young lion of the Secession, and its president who abandoned his classical historical duties as artist of the Ringstrasse to pursue a language for modern humankind that expressed misplaced truth. By not ignoring the classical structures totally, Klimt masterfully handled the ceilings of the University faculties of law, medicine, music, and philosophy—and so set the Secession style in European *Zeitgeist*. The Secessionists created a spandrel under which the future could recline into the present and proclaim the modern urban paradise.

Dreams, many might agree, allow us to experience things directly, leaving nothing out. Dreams are usually tolerable, sometimes helpful, often joyous. Problems can arise, however, in the frenetic interpretation of this realm of dreams, and Viennese generally have had the good taste not to peruse it. Dr. Freud's public struggle with inner and outer selves sought the ground for a scientific treatise in *The Interpretation of Dreams*. Vienna seemed to be both compelled and amused. The tenacious notion of *interpreting* rather than actually living out one's dreams struck the Viennese intellect as pretty dreamy itself: profound, elusive, unnecessary. Mind you, Viennese would never dream of contradicting Freud's interpretations, but they are likely to wonder why he takes it as seriously as he does.

> At the Café-Konditorei Gerstner in the Kärntner Strasse order Schwarzer—a cup of black coffee sometimes adding a little hot water, or Mocca Gespritzt—black coffee with cognac, or Melange—a small espresso served in a large cup with steamed milk or whipped cream.

Kinos are a Viennese favorite for nodding off, but the Artfilm always has found an accepting home in Vienna. Film in Vienna is supposed to live free from all other distractions and ready for democratic-humanist-conservatism that is safe from pedagogy, Benedictines, and communists. The cinema provides Viennese the visual images of the unimaginable. This continues, as many have found, even on leaving the cinema. Outside the Augustiner, in a flood of brilliant sunlight, perfect white stallions of the *Spanische Reitschule* cross Kohlmarkt near Michaelerplatz, on their way to the Hofburg Palace. Here, in the afternoon, is a manifest vision of horses, as Viennese have dreamed horses might be.

Young men who study philosophy in Vienna know that its underpinnings are myth and legend, and of the two, legend is the more organic. Intellectual Austria had entered the twentieth century with a model for urban modernization. The Ringstrasse, vestige of medieval consciousness, stronghold of Europe, acolyte of the national treasure, was the focus of philosophical Vienna. The Ringstrasse remains a self-contained carousel in which time moves through the Prehistoric to the Modern, to the Classical, then back to the Gothic. There is the Renaissance and its philhellenic overtones: early-, middle-, and late-outlandish Baroque. Important buildings imagined for modest sites were relocated on the Ringstrasse, in a remarkable sharing of aesthetic enthusiasm.

The variety of representational buildings arrayed along the Ring is testament to the modern Viennese celebration of the psychic states of humankind. The first and second estates are said to have dominated the inner spaces of the Ring: the Baroque Hofburg residence of the emperor—the visible expression of the aristocracy, and the Gothic Stephansdom that set the style for numerous smaller churches. From the attic window of the Naturhistorisches Museum, just where the Burg-Ring turns, it is possible to lean over the sill and look out on no century in particular to witness a magnificent parade: in the distance, the medieval spires of the Votivkirche; the Renaissance University, in homage to the true roots of modern secular learning; the Burgtheatre, in the style of the high Baroque; the massive Gothic Rathaus set at the rear of its own central park; and Parliament, given modern primacy in classical Greek.

> At the *Opern Café*, near the Albertina Platz try a *Schale Gold*—
> black coffee, adding cream until golden brown; or *Kapuziner* (like its
> Italian cousin come down from the Capucin monks)—a small cup
> of black coffee with a bit of cream, dressed with cocoa and finished
> with chocolate flakes.

Food serves approximately the same purpose in Vienna as elsewhere. Like most parts of the world, meat is incidental to the meal. There are many varieties of *kolbe, schnitzel,* and *kotellets* available, but they are not, in the Viennese mind, comparable to pastries—that is, a necessity. There is sausage, certainly, but this never really serves the same purpose as meat. It is the product of the butcher's tidying up in the *fleischmarkt* at the end of the day, more like a dream of meat.

American carnivores have always been well-advised to seek out the Italian or, failing that, the Hungarian restaurants first. Vienna survives well on its *kotofeln, spätzel,* and *knödeln* and, of course, its *käse*. There is far more gorgonzola and ementhaler purveyed at the Zwölf Apostlekeller to sustain its patrons than anything meaty. *Bierstüben* line the Ring on both sides but there has always been a livelier culture operating in the *Weinkellern*. Journeys to intellectual spaces are launched with *Weisswein, Rotwein, Dessertwein,* or a lovely warmed tincture of *Glüwein*.

Vienna is the birthplace of dissociation, with more or less equal forces of the arts and the academy. Americans really cannot comprehend the dissociative response. It is the moment when consciousness contracts the psychic equivalent of the hiccups. The subject slips into the hallucinatory crevice until a good deep breath arrives, and returns her or him once more to the avenue of liberal visions that support the general fantasy.

> *In Demel's, perhaps Europe's best-known café in the heart of Old Vienna, ask for the Einspänner ("one-horse carriage")—double espresso in a glass with a dollop of whipped cream, or the Mazagran—cold coffee served in a glass with maraschino, over crushed ice and clove.*

Vienna stands as evidence of the possibility of the modern. It is an Orphic city that undermines its loftiest thoughts with symbolic languages and has a lovely time doing it. It has boasted warriors, artists, physicists, and engineers who sought exacting truths. Vienna lived through them all.

Wittgenstein recommended that one consider ethics to be the same as aesthetics. Furthermore, he said the sense of the world must lie outside the world. This presumably means outside Vienna as well. However, this proposition is found in his *Tractatus Logico-Philosophicus*, which, like the waltz, proves on close examination to have no reason.

For all that life leaves out, the curiously implausible remains attractive just for its being so unlikely. Ecstasy is inauthentic—ingenious enterprise rails constantly against destiny. No, the truth of the natural world comes in dreams. Dreamers then dress them up sometimes in legend so as to keep them going once everyone is awake. Master commentators on disintegration have for a century described *fin-de-siècle* Austria as full of movement not knowing what it was moving toward. Vienna keeps time in a kind of Apollonian tomb with easy access and all the amenities.

CHAPTER THIRTEEN

Café Vandal

Courage is the price that life exacts for granting peace.
— Amelia Earhart

In the dim light of the small venues of Old Europe, it's often hard to make out the American expatriate jazz players, even when they are the feature attraction. It's hard to make out anything—harder still to see what the patrons thought they were coming to hear. Watching in the dark, they wait in anonymous comfort for destiny to take charge and fill their little panorama. This is the real attraction of small gathering places; they encourage small destinies that fit in the room. Perhaps the musician imagines he is playing to a gathering that appreciates what he is laying down for them. They, in turn, imagine they are digging it.

Gathering in such places has always carried with it, danger. Lessons linger in the air, that danger comes with being a westerner, a pretender to sophistication and easy convert to the cultural trend. Opulence carries with it mortal danger. There is danger in a misdirected kindness. Intellectuals are forever in danger.

It is often dangerous to be one of the barbarians but usually fatal to be opposed to them. What has lasted so long in this part of the world, in Eastern Europe, is an array of eclectic behavior that summons its chameleon deconstructions whenever it is necessary to cover its finest feathers. The ability to become anything else for a while was born and perfected in this part of the world. Romantic fledglings from America came face to face, in large numbers, with what Mark Twain saw as "a community of fossils, ancient things that had become something else holding onto their own atavist image."

Innocents abroad can never be prepared for the quiet violence done to the soul by gazing into the unexpected lowness of humankind. Strange how the intellect disguises itself to preserve what it needs. What is visible is paradox, and paradox has always been preferred to danger. Many regions of Eastern Europe continue a hasty burlesque and feverish carnival filled with masked fossils, none of whom is wearing her own clothes. Beauty is regarded as disease, kindly monks are bent on the military way, perfection is saluted in the disintegration of order, the harlequin distills happiness from the future—pouring it on the floor. Misfortune comes in the light of a new day, and it is simply too late for suicide.

How foreign this is to the dominant American Anglo-Saxon stock, whose folkways have institutionalized our own national hypocrisies. Teutons instinctively understand, but their strain has long since been diluted in America by the Celts. So the idea of American eminence is characterized, at its loftiest, as merely outlandish. Americans cannot fully participate in the parade of civilizations; for we have no aristocracy, at least most of the "united states" can show nothing that would qualify. Americans may lack the right perspective and sense of drama. It has been suggested that there never was an aristocrat born north of Baltimore. H.L. Mencken, who would not sit still for being in the same sentence with an aristocrat, held that American civilization was at its lowest "precisely in those areas where the Anglo Saxon still presumed to rule."

By virtue of an ability to redirect the emotions of the mob to nearly always profitable ends, Americans have an odd kinship with the eastern part of Europe. Beyond the boredom of wanton destruction there is for Americans a certain appeal and a willing acceptance of vandalism. The appeal is not so much rooted in the European notion of the vandal as feared metaphysical agent of purification but more in the *counter-bourgeois* vandal as a numb apostle of empty-headedness.

It is in the heart of Europe that westerners have always been surprised to find themselves. Prized since antiquity for its many attractions and wealth accumulated by the beneficent geography that set it along the oldest trade routes, this region sits as a mysterious Helleno-Asiatic hybrid filled to capacity with legend and dark memory. Yet there is an oddly familiar air of being at home in a land susceptible to the infection of opinions. Many opinions are ancient, and some are unsettling. At the gateway to India and China, there has always been the daily wait for unforeseen despair and manifold varieties of dread. Deep in the east of Europe, Hamlet is an optimist, the saints are blasé and apathetic to pleasure or excitement, and everyone is defined by his anxiety and distress. Europe's brilliance is concentrated here, along with its discomforts, in what we call "Eastern Europe."

Among its riches is amber, a fossil valued in early times. Though found along the shores of the Baltic and North Sea, the great amber-producing country historically has been the Samland promontory of East Prussia. Pieces of amber torn from the sea floor are cast up by the waves to be collected at ebb tide. Its burnished color is re-animated by a static electricity charge, like gold, having some life under its inviting surface but remaining inaccessible.

For centuries everyone wanted some. Relics of amber have been found in Mycenaean tombs. Turks regarded amber as especially valuable. When fashioned into pipe mouthpieces it is virtually incapable of transmitting infection when passed from mouth to mouth. Trade in amber has left the marks of its wide distribution, extending over a large part of northern Europe to the Urals. Baltic amber was well known in prehistory and, like most things of value that have emerged in this land, the best qualities were sent to Vienna.

Between the Amber Road and Roman Africa, tiny taverns have been populated by old men who tell humorous stories and share philosophies. No one listens. Boredom has given into its own cure of stupor and, in the words of the poet, anyone who ends in the morgue cannot be judged a failure. There is a lot of waiting to do here. Deliverance is a complicated affair.

Eastern Europe exhibits a characteristic sagacity and a self-repudiation, enjoyed as the pastime of many nations. Conversation is the currency, and life is spiked with mischief and villainy. There are a dozen or so nationalities and, of course, many more who have not recognized any of the others. The slurry of nostalgia is for something that is neither East, nor West—but somehow German, Austrian, Magyar, Hungarian, Croat, Czech, Hungarian, Romanian, Bulgarian, Slav, Bohemian, Polish, Pomeranian, Dacian, Thracian, Dalmatian. Universal union of these beautiful and wild places lives on as the idea of "Transylvania," a cultural metaphor stretched over a state of mind. It is the product of the other symbol of Eastern Europe: the tortured intellectual. This old habit gives rise to a conversational din of numberless dialogues.

The birth of vandalism was an extended event that occurred between the Juras and the Black Sea, from Scandinavia to Alexandria. Each city or village needed to keep its own sense of peace and security if it was to enjoy growth and prosperity between waves of vandals. Budapest is such an argument for the synthesis of cultures that would hold off the vandals. It flowered as something orderly and enduring in the exuberant intellectual life of 1900, lived out in six hundred cafés. With its factories, railhead and architectural palaces, it was a Chicago set in the middle of the road that connected Occident with Orient. A great capacity for self-renewal has repeatedly been given the chance to demonstrate itself owing to unimaginable damage it has sustained in its dark Hungarian destiny of misery. The three ancient cities—Buda, Pest and Obuda (even older Buda)—were united only in 1873. As partner in the Dual Monarchy, Budapest (like Chicago) was on a path of expansion powered by immigrants. Slovenes, as it turned out— seeing less opportunity under German, Greek, and Jewish entrepreneurs—ended up in Chicago with yet another state language.

Eastern Europe is highly conscious of class. Apart from language, it is seen in the panorama from the Buda side, rising above the steep terraces to patrician Castle Hill and falling off behind to ancient districts of tradesmen and artisans. On the Pest shore there have been grand hotels and large public buildings. But farther in from the Danube, and for many centuries, have sat the ghettos and a poverty more Eastern than Western. Winged Hussars embody the magic quality of Hungary. Nobility endures in the mind, even where aristocrats and laborers relish the same national dishes. For strange and distorted images of national memory, however, Hungarians must yield to the Poles.

In recurrent hibernation, Poland holds onto its description as a land where a man can make a success of himself and make a shambles of his country. Its history is both awesome and all over the place. Spanning the best agricultural soil from the River Oder to the Dneiper, Polish land expands and contracts through history with its own intense self-direction, like breathing in the dark. A millennium ago, the first Poland was that of the Piast Dynasty. Slavic peoples of the fields, the *Polanie*, put together a loose confederation along the Vistula in order to resist German expansion to the east. These lands were prosperous. There were frequent visits by other barbarians. The last Piast was Casimir the Great, who oversaw Poland as the easternmost outpost of Christianity. Ever since, the Poles have tried a more peaceful approach to evangelism. The sparkling apex for Poland is really the story of Lithuania, the last pagans of Europe.

Teutonic crusaders had reached Danzig and were threatening when they hit resistance. The Lithuanians preferred to eventually accept peaceful baptism at the hands of the Poles and, together, the two nations broke Teutonic power at the Battle of Tannenberg in 1410, which secured Prussia once more as a vassal of Poland. We seize upon the *mazurka* as a symbol of modern Poland. The lesson from Poland that Americans have taken to heart, however, is that for a nation to be both daring and weak is dangerous.

Bygone splendor is a big part of the compensation of Eastern Europe. Small principalities periodically re-asserting the suzerain of an ancient duchy are indeed splendid. The whole of Czech culture was eliminated for two hundred years at the hands of Catholic Bohemia but comes down to us today in a mixed lore of the life of St. Wenceslaus. Eastern Europe is a serious objective for Americans. This is no empire of the ephemeral self the likes of Athens and Venice. Rather this is the region where life is destroyed by consciousness. There is no lyricism without frenzy here in the realm of castles and homeless poets. At a glance it seems to the westerner that the great river systems have defined political geography. Easterly flows the Danube linking many capitals cities and centers of fun. There is also the Elbe, the Oder, and the Vistula (of Gdansk, Warsaw, and Kraków) running south and north—and the Tisza, Dnieper, Dniester, and Don. Trade has been critical but plunder has had the last word.

In its earlier identity, Eastern Europe has entailed a basic confusion of adhering either to Roman or Byzantine visions. This has been concentrated in Western Europe to its woe and is seen by the West, and particularly by Americans, as a passion to condense all its rich cultural diversity into orderly, attractive, sweet-smelling co-existence. Eastern Europeans, in Mencken's words, "smell flowers and look around for the funeral." Union of culture here, as elsewhere, has meant the disappearance of something. Folk stories of the Czechs, Poles, Slovaks, Hungarians, and Bohemians are fragmented, turbulent, and brutal. Hemmed in by larger powers, much of their energy has been spent on preserving language—that most-visible possession that also is most obscure and despised. Bucharest, Prague, Sofia, and Belgrade together formed at the beginning of this century perhaps the greatest cultural centers for literature, graphics, and the performing and dramatic arts. The contribution of the vandals has been to demonstrate that, while weak states can survive for a time, civilization includes things that are lasting. Institutions have to be built, then maintained and protected. This precept dates back to the earliest legends of the Goths and Lombards, both of whom encountered the East Germanic tribes of Vandals unsuccessfully.

Vandals systematically emptied Europe's great centers of all movable treasures and holy vessels, anointing themselves *Sacristans of the Valuable Object*. They held up a portrait of life completely bereft of anything that endures. It is a relief that this is not to everyone's liking. Yet there was nobility—not the nobility of the institution, but a personal nobility. A certain combination of self-restraint, moderation, clemency, and maturation of character was allied with courage and resolve. Civilization thus was encouraged, and the marauders disappeared in history. Transience carries with it the air of possibility. Eastern Europe has endured by creative energy and with it a proclivity for the grandiloquent.

Americans have carried their affections to the hesitating heart of Europe. What they have seen in recent decades has mirrored the sharp and rapid delineations of character depicted in human nature. Intellectual vandalism has been worn in various fashions as part of the national dress of a dozen countries. This part of Europe, in its forty-four-year flirtation with communism, struggled with factious citizenries. Pragmatic traditions of camouflage and subterfuge had worked. Playwrights and poets had become heads of state. Faced with radical change, memory frequently outweighs knowledge and reason put together. Tendencies toward doom revive. Hungarian intellectual and literary vandal, John Lukacs, once published a personal note: "Europe is my mother. America is my wife."

Guileless American travelers bent on Eastern Europe found themselves down to their last piastre in Stara Zagora and on the verge of insight. So thoroughly has the American product penetrated foreign nations that the sin is evident. No country accounts for a greater part of what is now accepted as the common cultural inheritance of humankind. Eastern Europe regards Americans and thinks them good, and productive—perhaps not virtuous, certainly not noble—but inventive, naïve, and affable. Americans, however, are seen as consistently electing populist governments that put everyone else in danger. This, of course, is in the spirit of the leather-jacketed American vandal that can be seen reproduced on street corners of Tokyo, Buenos Aires, and anywhere there is a rising economic class.

It was inevitable that these nationalities once more become the broken heart of Europe. Native exports include transients and those fugitives from systematic intolerance. They look back from the New World, longing for that romantic land they have been able to construct in their exiled minds. Newspapers serving European nationalities in the United States find their readers are aging and it is difficult to attract younger ones. Many second and third generation Germans and Poles grow up speaking little of the language of home. Still, just under a million readers, Armenian to Yiddish, look to the foreign-language press and closely examine the *Abend-Post* or *Dziennik Polski*.

Writing home to his *Daily Alta California* in San Francisco, Mark Twain kept a journal as the new barbarian at the ruins of antiquity. Twain's letters don't so much raise interest in Europe as they dispel the mythology surrounding the place. His vision and adventures are the next best thing. Only seeing Europe firsthand can do more to debunk it. He should be read for affirmation after the experience rather than for inspiration before it.

Eastern Europeans find one barbaric quality irresistible: overcoming that primal human emotion—fear. The American who puts his business in the street, as if it didn't matter, crosses a universal frontier of danger. This impresses, and at the same time comforts, observers in the east end of Europe and gives them ideas. Americans showed little respect and no fear in creating jazz, then living it out. Eastern Europeans, in the words of one jazz trumpeter, "like the idea of jazz." After the war, they filled Amerika Haus in Frankfurt and many other centers, to listen to

Chet Baker and Thelonius Monk. They happily lose years in the café, contemplating bravado, awaiting the vandals' next set.

CHAPTER FOURTEEN

Doctrine's Orders

*Our lives are merely strange dark interludes
in the electrical display.*
— Eugene O'Neill

Empire runs its course. No matter that empire is all bound up in ideas of itself as cohesive and permanent. It is by nature a transitory thing. The inevitability of empire's passing is recognized in its strongest feature, namely, memory of it. Well into the sixteenth century, in the great hall of the Knights of the Golden Fleece in Brussels, the Emperor Charles V abdicated his many thrones and signaled the passing of the medieval world order. It was passing to Philip, now King of Spain, the Americas, the Netherlands, and a few other places including England, whose queen, Bloody Mary, he had recently wed.

Philip did not share his father's practical nature; by most reports he exhibited other qualities. He was petulant, crafty, ideological. His own mission, he believed, was to restore the absolute rule of the Roman Church, and from the most powerful throne in Europe he used gold and silver from Peru to send armies of the Inquisition to the Low Countries.

Not even the riches of America, however, would suffice in Philip's war. For a while the idea of heresy was forgotten, and Holland presently became the symbol of tolerance and civility. Descendants of the Dutch sailed for what would become New York. In our own century, many remember the British Empire. At its zenith, it had dominion over a fifth of the land surface, one-quarter of the people, and all the oceans and seas in between. The peace that followed the Second World War—a peace none welcomed more than the British—witnessed a rising tide of secession. Awakening nationalism created a potent liquidation of former colonial holdings. What one eloquent historian wryly described as the "lion's share" dwindled to a mere seventeen members in the British Commonwealth of Nations.

It has been surprising, if not altogether unexpected, that in the span of a generation the doctrine of empire was transformed into the doctrine of democratic-social development. The twentieth century's first generation had to rebuild the world after the Great War; the next had to rebuild that new world just revived from the Great Depression. Somewhere, the changing force of empire became the battle for men's and women's minds. As far as the third generation was concerned, this meant the battle for personal fulfillment.

Some sense of history then gripped students at American colleges and universities. On any given day, critical thinking was being applied to news of assorted mandarins having been exposed or denounced here and there for horrid mistreatment of entire countries. Many thought the world probably could try a little harder. The young would correct as many of these mammoth mistakes as possible, past and present, through purifying acts of participation in big and small international affairs.

An enormous political vehicle pulled up to mobilize this spirit. A big idea took shape that would harness the skills, enthusiasm, and global awareness rife in post-collegiate ranks and put it into some productive use for them and others. The topic was international development and cooperation supported by the nearly free labor of a vast corps of emergent voters. By the time the political class assessed its possibilities and took hold of the idea, it had been named the "Peace Corps."

The Peace Corps was essentially designed for the volunteer bent on experience and eager to round out her or his education. The experience would provide a not-totally-unvarnished picture that would lead to broader understanding. Any economic gains or elevation in the local standard of living in developing areas would be a dividend. Decades later there was almost no real effect. Instead, the benefit for developing areas would be very far down the road. It would come in terms of American insight, awareness, and perhaps some of that broader understanding. It might eventually influence who went to Congress—how they voted on the foreign aid budget. Peace Corps volunteers went into paradise and there observed oppression and disease. The experience would give them a fuller understanding of the Hindu description of heroism, "endurance for one moment longer."

Circulating in the developing world meant one must forge a new American view and live according to a counter-political doctrine. In doctrinaire fashion, the media had classified most areas of the world for us. For the American in-country, however, doctrine was to be supplanted by the myths of the village and memory of forebears that project the living in time.

To the ancestors of the Inca kings, the supreme creator of the universe first appeared in the sapphire waters surrounding the sacred rock of Iticaca, the island oracle to the Aymara philosopher-priests. The sun's rays touched the island, illuminating the peoples of the world, drawing them away from their rough conditions. Following legend, the Inca kings were indeed believed to be "children of the sun"—in mystical cooperation and intimate participation with the gods.

Young Americans placed in remote locales learned quickly that villages do not exist without myth. In Bolivia and Peru, the profound myths, like that of Supreme Creator Viracocha, have been described as projecting themselves in time—in their way making the future secure and familiar. Peace Corps volunteers found corresponding traditions in Jamaica, Haiti, Ethiopia, India, and Korea.

Many questioned why the United States, and Canada for that matter, were so much more affluent, democratic, and stable. Both these northern countries seemed to have begun from a point of ethics rather than culture. There was no real clash of contrasting visions of life at the point their democratic systems were established. To be sure, there was overrunning of native populations and annihilation of cultural traditions, but this is not the same thing as social change. North American democracies began pragmatically. Dominant motives were ethical not cultural. They were simple and primary.

First was *safety*. Once safe, the people could move on to *self-reliance*, together with a sense of predictability in life.

Characteristics of this unique evolution have been identified as *American*, for they are rare and fleeting in other places—these qualities of tolerance and stability.

In one contrasting view, Bolivia remains a dramatic country and La Paz is its climax. Half-finished buildings in its center show a city trying to become what someone in the development community thinks a modern Bolivian capital should be. It stands as the sum of its constituent free-market parts. No one lives there. All its people are balanced on the steep surrounding hillsides. *Laderas* exist in a makeshift present, the timeless peak of Illimani on the horizon. Many appropriate electricity from construction sites and live somehow in possibility. They look down on empty shells of new buildings that will eventually need people in them.

American witnesses to international development wanted to extend to others the concept of wellbeing guided by the notion of safety and predicated on practical reason. These were actually inherited ideas, having come from Germans, Dutch, Swedes, English, Scots—in fact, most of Philip's empire.

Doctrinaire thinking had given us the uncomfortable notion that the political stability enjoyed by the US was supported by a system of Whigs and Marxists. America's new idea was precisely this: to involve Americans (or at least a small, rarefied substrate of them) in foreign policy at a level where they thought they were experiencing change, sometimes having hallucinations in which they were invoking it.

That Marxist-socialist doctrines have not helped much in developing areas is no endorsement of capitalism, which understandably has been identified with exploitation of the past rather than with free enterprise of the future. Comically incompetent government, financial mismanagement, and illogical visions of daily life continue to greet the curious traveler, who also may run into the French, Dutch, and Chinese mineral rights dealer. Commerce is immune from ethics in these regions. As long as money is changing hands, it represents potential, at least for those who have some. The horrifying chronicle of countless development projects is filled with the dull boorishness of those who believe capitalism is a form of government and the foolish bureaucrats who think it's not.

Equatorial and tropical environments present obstacles to economic development, even where local society has thrived. When so many common factors are present in regions of low productivity, it's difficult to pin down the overriding cause: devastating disease, inadequate rainfall, unfathomable religious incongruence, ignorance, upheaval, bad habits. Late-twentieth-century understanding of prominent ideologies has come out of the mist, codified by academics and scholarly ponderers and passed on to other professional cynics who continue to endorse and perpetuate the accepted view.

It was necessary for Americans serving in manifold internships to have some rough appreciation of political doctrine in order that they might quickly learn something from their experience. Common renditions were heard by dozing audiences subjected to the development-expert after-dinner speaker. One version describes things this way—

Socialism: *you have two cows—you give one to your neighbor.*

Communism: *you have two cows—the government takes both of them and gives you milk.*

Fascism: *you have two cows—the government takes both of them and sells you milk.*

Nazism: *you have two cows—the government takes both of them and shoots you.*

Bureaucracy: *you have two cows—the government takes both of them, shoots one, milks the other, and pours the milk down the drain.*

Capitalism: *you have two cows—you sell one of them and buy a bull.*

So much of our planet exercises its right to long for a world free of the pernicious dominance of the United States. Yet the American hemisphere is bound by myths of empire and the mire of development.

The name *America* is a compromise, a word holding no intrinsic meaning. Early on, some had thought to call the country "Columbia" in honor of Columbus—*who died without knowing the continent existed.* However, during the national debate the old viceroyalty of New Granada, south of the Rio Grande, took the name Colombia. In a burst of desperate creativity, it then was suggested the country be christened *the nation of freedom*. Anglo-Saxon root combined with Greco-Latin ending to produce "Freedonia." Almost immediately it was pointed out that in view of a strong Spanish influence, there was every chance that Spanish literalists would lean heavily on the phonetic *doña* and promulgate this as *the land of loose ladies.*

For a while there was no proper name for this place. Now less than half the hemisphere identifies itself as American. There are Hispano Americans of Honduras, Portuguese Americans of Brazil. America is the New Spain of Cortéz, the New France of Cartier, the New Albion of no one in particular. America had begun as a state of mind and became the new concept for civil life. The transforming doctrine coming out of the northern American hemisphere had to do with the feeling of liberty. In the southern hemisphere, it would be instead a passion for invention of unrealities.

Latin America consistently resists the sort of pluralistic social success the *Nortes* offer up. There is also a purification through literature, parts of which circulate northward on hemispheric breezes. Literature in modern Latin America has often been marked by horror and elegance, fables read as possibility, unworldly interior landscapes, and curious new alphabets. Argentine Jorge Luis Borges; Gabriel García Márquez of Colombia; Peru's Mario Vargas Llosa; Carlos Fuentes, blending Europe with México; and Víctor Jara of Chile have each contributed some personal vision of magic and anarchy that applies to no specific century.

This diet has customarily been difficult for North Americans to digest. Some are drawn to it but end up taking unreality to be a riddle. This is often fatal. Misanthrope newspaperman Ambrose Bierce may have reckoned it suicide from the beginning, but it is equally plausible that the American satirist and lexicographer became lost in the personalization of morality and, by legend, simply disappeared somewhere in Coahuila.

The thoroughfare of morality, every American since Bierce knows, is not found on the US highway atlas. It is outside the borders. Ancient teachings say it is the Zen path that begins as the road out of town and ends in a *passe-partout*—a master key for the subject to unlock his or her experience.

Young Americans took Bierce's mental itinerary in all directions. One course created its own folklore as the "hippie trail," pointing east in the direction of Hermann Hesse. On the trail, those repentant of their life of privilege would learn the doctrines of the righteous heart and the radiant mind. They would learn how to properly perform holy sacrifices. The doctrine is, if not Hindu, very old. It says there are evil results from getting desirable things from an undesirable source.

These are the Sanskrit roots of Peace Corps doctrine that say the search for all forms of wealth is attended by danger. No one attains her or his fortune without embarking on adventure.

At the same time, no one has argued with the suggestion that the hippie trail closely followed the spread of empire, from north and west to south and east. Mythology in the East is different than in the West. It still is a great part of Eastern living at every level. Aryans on the hippie trail in the second millennium BCE never settled anywhere for long. What we know of these first Aryan agents of development, bringers of bronze and cultivators of the valleys, we read in the Vedic hymns.

A hundred thousand years ago the tear-drop-shaped land of the Sinhalese, the "lion people," separated from the subcontinent. Sri Lanka's legacy has been the spiritual gifts it continues to offer humankind. The pathway that reverses the logic of development and offers the sophisticated West a complementary universe, leads to Sri Lanka and traditional Hindu cosmology. This is the unaltered and continuous doctrine.

Those who survived the trail know something about the human yearning for progress and desire to make *terra nostra* from the dim ignorance of *terra incognita*. There is essential learning around how change strongly reverts to culture wherever it can find it. Still it's clear that reordering doctrine eventually goes the way of empire.

CHAPTER FIFTEEN

Supreme Futures

I've seed de first en de last…
I seed de beginning, en now I sees de endin.
— William Faulkner

Soaring like a dove, high on the glide and far above the earth, is an old Greek idea. To see clearly where one *is* and especially where one *is headed* has for centuries been a glorious notion rich in human possibility. As with most ideas of the ancients, Plato improved upon it. For him, the metaphorical dove floated not only unfettered, but in a vacuum—frictionless. Not only seeing but understanding, it was loose from constraints and beyond the grasp of time. The ancient appeal was the promise of knowing the future by suddenly seeing everything.

Contemplating the future in any active way implies that it's possible to make some little difference. All those dramas based on misinterpretation, falsity, and neglect of the future set the ancients wondering if they could better their lot through anticipation, compassion, and reason. For Plato, tragic drama was a faint and imperfect allegory—a misleading metaphor. Limits placed on the future, he thought, may be fashioned in the mind, but they are also part of our very nature. Sense of identity and possibilities, in any modern understanding, probably began with the great impact science had as a way of knowing the future. To calculate upon the yet-to-be was to predict what would happen. This, of course, changes the idea of future. Numerous and valuable discoveries and inventions of the eighteenth century—vaccination, the sextant, the chronometer, the steam condenser—quickly became essential to our understanding not only of what was coming but what had always been there right in front of us.

Some found this perfectibility of humankind a contemptible idea. They were skeptical, if not downright scornful, about science in general. From Swift and Defoe—to Jules Verne and H.G. Wells, skeptical futurists brought readers out of the world and into questionable utopias of the mind, at the same time challenging them to disprove finite possibility.

In some variations this meant Poe taking humanity galactic ballooning to observe the vast secrets held in the future. Imaginary trips in fantastic airships both free and nourish the spirit by loosening earthly bonds. Floating in a platonic vacuum, the view in front of the eyes is wide enough to include the future.

Even sitting here on the ground, the future is coming this way. The marriage of liberal visions to restless energy has established many a public works project that defines where we think we are and what we want to leave behind. Galvanizing ideas are what have brought many civilizations toward some edition of the future, once leadership has convinced the laborers that the high priests have thought of everything. Then all can participate with the comfort that, no matter what languages they speak or the strange and wonderful ways they do things in the future, they are now yoked to it and therefore cannot be vanquished or convicted. State visions have traditionally required material monuments. They survive all around us.

Stonehenge was raised according to some remote and mystical vision about four thousand years ago. Massive trilithons hold enigmatic lintels high above the earth. Merlin, so the legend goes, floated bluestones from the Preseli Hills of Wales into the gaunt circle of Sarsen stones on the Wiltshire plain. Over the centuries, humankind has taken the ancient future of Merlin and re-cast it in its own view of tomorrow. In this view, white-robed Druids gathered at the midsummer sunrise and modern Britons talk of these petrified giants dancing, hands on each other's shoulders. All eighty stones probably did float down the Severn and the inland riverway, where many participants cut and dressed them, then hauled them into the future.

Petra likewise seems always to have been there, thrust into the future in the early days of time in silken colors of some other world that will come again. The citadel of Machu Pichu pierces the future as it hangs in suspense among Andean peaks. It is a spectacle viewed from Earth with a gaze directly upward and ahead.

The paradise that lies in tomorrow has been reflected many times in different fashions—the Shwedagon Pagoda of Yangon, Justinian's Hagia Sophia, the thousand-eyed Potala of the Dalai Lama. That the future is a mystery to be known only by the most privileged is the deep secret of labyrinthine Topkapi Palace and the dazzling image of the fourteenth century's version, the Alhambra. Great Khan's Pleasure Dome of Xanadu may have gotten a little out of hand, as futures were going in the thirteenth century, begetting the Forbidden City, on which the sun of the future shines. Not a single temple but a purposive view of the cosmos, the Imperial City is laid out, like Chang'An before it, in the center of the present so that the winds and seas continually bring it to its symbolic order with the universe.

In these projects, there is always democratic participation, for it is only the body that is forbidden entry. The spirit moves to the innermost chambers and from this same terrestrial prospect; like legendary Viking warrior Holger the Dane, sleeping in the dark cellar of Kronborg Castle at Helsingør, all lapidaries dream themselves into the future.

Monarchs, moguls, and the Maya have all been guilty of the sort of imperial hoarding that weakens the state's grip on the present in order to secure a divine future for the anointed few. Public works projects of this supreme magnitude give many examples of the big idea as it is handled by the state. All seem to be founded on the same kind of engineering solution to the problem of place and the need for a meaningful sense of the present.

Another common feature of all these glories is that each one was erected while Holger the Dane was contemplating the unthinkable: perhaps there is no future. In fact, futures can be divided along such lines of— on the one hand, the Delphian Oracle, a municipal service available to champions and heroes but also to the merely earnest and inquisitive—and on the other, the Great Pyramid, the end for many a disenfranchised laborer having no interest whatsoever in a single additional tomorrow. Lofty visions and otherworldly sacred concepts are what modern government needs to do its best to avoid.

To the post-apocalyptic/retro-holocaust/negative/modern/utopian sensibility, the future belongs to science, and that's fine. It is pleasing, in an agreeable, pseudo-productive way, to accept that times to come will be chock full of: artifact coding, replicators, planetary engineering, space-time control consoles managing publicly-funded black hole trials, world mind, and immortality. The unsettling thing is that states with high levels of energy, capital, and a sense of the continuum feel obliged to make some type of lasting work, when the era of the material monument is passing away.

The premise of science is eventually to exhaust the unknown. Any possible future demands to be contemplated with both nerve and imagination. Twentieth-century western governments have shown plenty of one and not nearly enough of the other. It's just plain debilitating to conclude that the future really belongs to bacteria or insects, and that humans have only the meager skills to postpone for a few million years their own miserable end.

Generations must teach themselves virtue and continually define the fields of experience that lie ahead. There certainly are specious acts of creativity and substitute adventures, and these distractions are real. Both nerve and imagination in turn become institutions with a constant value and universal access. Standards are raised with each exceptional act of courage and creativity. What progress is made usually comes with one individual convincing another that there is a new and exciting version of understanding, action, and responsibility available to all of us.

All societies seem to acquire their best features through questionable means. Everything is borrowed, stolen, or made-up in a revisionist's construction and the forgeries of a thief. A society that counts activism among its virtues wants to get on with it. It wants to establish inspiring conditions and some clever juggling of Providence.

Seeing the Great Pyramid as a gigantic symbol of an alien mentality gives us an incomplete and misleading view. Science volunteers that the future of the pyramid is reduced by the half-life of the protons that make it up. Societies that radiate the future, however, seem to have recognized the twin forces of unity and diffusion that are in play. It becomes easy then to see the pyramid as awkward on land (like so many magnificent creations) but perfection as a spiritual conveyance moving to the far-distant nucleus of the situation.

In our individual cosmologies, many who habitually harbor less confidence in tomorrow long for the incandescent spirit that reaches through the high vacuum and places us gently on the soaring dove.

4

BOOK OF VISIONS

Reliving decades of the eighties and nineties…

Architecture creates horizons it then breaks through, building a bridge to what comes next.

Everything on television is delivered through an American prism that creates a cool place of the imagination.

Native peoples spoke of comprehending everything in a single lifetime in a universal vision with a whiff of destiny.

Physicist and ballplayer agree that the center of the universe is relative, and "it's not the matter, it's the field."

The twinkling of American philosophy is liberty held in the joyful flow of undirected thought and the logic of change.

CHAPTER SIXTEEN

National Endowments

> *I was a little disappointed on receiving your
> rather lengthy letter to find no mention of money.*
> — Groucho Marx

If indeed it's natural to feel that things should be getting better, then progress often seems to be drawn away by many distractions. Every day should contain a sprinkling of humor, and some days bring the faint aroma of truth. This makes things seem complete, but it is inadequate. Most Americans look to improve.

In all this movement, many have looked to artists to pin down intuitive and unconscious notions to identify what's important. An inner sense of fitness, success, and belonging is made sensible through the work of the poet and the pastry chef. This has brought many Americans to the city.

Cities make up a rather large part of the historical record. They happen by design or through collections of things. They offer accommodations but also compress events, making them part of the masonry. Working with a fine stylus, an architect scratches out trenchant comments in arching structures that separate one thing from everything else. That too many architects appear to be using blunt instruments against their own murky, paranoid visions is proved by the wide array of interpreted plazas, buildings, and even entire cities blighting the horizon.

Architecture possesses two qualities every art owns. First, somebody finds it unattractive—and second, it does something *for* us as we do something *with* it. Some cities think they have more architecture than others, but everyone owns every part of architecture together, tenants-in-the-entirety. Its faculties as structures in space enable architecture to overcome spatial distance. Architecture creates horizons, then it breaks through.

Good architects of our time are adept at being conscious of what was in a place before the first building went up. This sensibility separates architects from other artists—not the fact that they are conscious, but that they must develop a useful sense of the flow of time. They cause something to be placed that has its own *time-less-ness* even as it is complementary to the present tense. Anxiety is good for good architects. A sense of what was there before is certainly possessed by most sculptors as well. The exalted position mediocrity achieved at what some critic thought to call the close of the *modern* set other critics to naming what would come afterward. They called it "postmodern."

The big idea of postmodernism has several attributes that are especially American, in that it formed as a response to the movement of scientific certainty and the possibility of an objective reality. In this way the postmodern proposition also describes American culture in its skeptical approach. The term has been applied to literature, philosophy, and culture itself—but it is architecture that is so hard to ignore.

Defining the postmodernist was not so simple as naming one, and architects shared that task of identifying some more practical reason for having something after the modern. In fact, architects are a reasonable choice for this purpose; they can usually be located, and are objective and audacious. They are accustomed to ignorance and know the committee process. They are untainted by herds of benighted collectors. Their work is not easily moved. They must have a philosophy. They need to provide answers.

Planetary life may be divided into the horizontal and vertical of individual landscapes. Each individual is broadened, elevated, and enriched by the ideas dominating late-twentieth-century architecture, namely the conversation of organic with inorganic in the play of light and freedom of space. Nothing is there to mediate architecture. Goethe wrote to someone, "architecture is frozen music," but this does not at all guarantee its sublime aspect. In fact, some postmodernists acknowledge that much of music is just there, like air conditioning.

Clues to the postmodern emerge from the architectural education that teaches us new architecture is a wholeness prepared of technologies outside a subjective world. Art in its postmodern architectural flavors refers to knowledge derived from nature—not observation but presence in and association with it. In this sense, postmodernism begins with buildings that create a new horizon. Architectural education in the twentieth century came first to Germans, who instinctively understand these things. Americans, however, advanced the notion in cities, and the postmodern arrived with its supplicants. Yet while architecture seems to have the virtue of being able to explain more, it also demands something. Architecture is art we live in.

The encrypted term "postmodernist" appeared sometime in 1930s America as a rather uninviting description of the coded bunch of styles forming a new eclecticism. Architecture provided a center of gravity. It insisted that there were manifold *concrete* (also steel and glass) solutions for the deconstructed problems of contemporary human living.

Postmodernism, as seen through architectural experience, actually began with the Bauhaus and the personalities of Gropius, Klee, Le Corbusier, and Mies van der Rohe. American Frank Lloyd Wright made the idea of a new sort of rationalism an organic one. He moved toward essential principles of unity bound up in nature. Architecture occurs only when its own immanent laws crystallize and stand up in a structural argument in which people can sit down.

The possessed energy of the postmodern surfaced the problem of just how an individual relates to the object at hand. If architecture is our key to experience, many will accept Le Corbusier's characterization of architecture as the "pure creation of mind." Insistence on traditional rationalist thinking suggests what postmodernist architecture celebrates. Architects plan for a back door to the past. Pleasure comes in relating to objects historically.

So why can't a brilliant architect build a city? Someone's universal law says that genius is no guarantee of comprehensiveness. A city of the postmodern era needs something else. Kept aloft by its own anxiety, it debates whether material progress is nobler than transient purpose and whether there ever is one without the other. A postmodernist building argues with its neighbors. So many parts of cities have been constructed using hypnosis that it is dangerous to let anyone's subjective imagination get too close. Even ordinary city squares mount new drama in bad weather, and the city's blood pressure rises and falls in the traffic of its sidewalks.

Differences between the grammars of art and architecture probably outnumber their likenesses, but each movement must establish its own physics—its way of dealing with time and space. There need to be rules for finding the way in new worlds. When postmodernism invites someone to slip out the back door, the energy is heady for some, befuddling to others. In the postmodern moment, the subject is in a state of suspension that accommodates a variety of nervous conditions.

Logic brought postmodernism, then it left. Ludwig Mies van der Rohe made logic and truth real in the Barcelona Pavilion of 1926. He brought it back in 1958 with his universal statement of technology in the service of ideas, the Seagram Building. There is an absolute principle in his architecture that is independent of the senses which bring it. Mies's ideas may have been derived from his medieval studies, through the back door.

At the same time, America accepted Frank Lloyd Wright's view of himself as "earth-son." His skyscrapers were trees, his houses caves—and that structure built to house postmodern abstract art, the museum, was the shape of an ancient nautilus. Wright saw integrity operating everywhere. The artist was spiritual giver of the matrix for civilization, and the architect *is* the artist. Everything Wright destroyed in Taliesin West (Welsh for "shining brow") and Fallingwater he did quietly in organic tranquility, as if Copland were being played in the background and Nature was surely pleased. Genius abides in postmodern visitations of the abstract and in the unfolding of architectural space.

The postmodern arrived as the first era that looked backward to prior generations. Unlike the post-impressionist, for example, it is more like post-apocalyptic. The logic of Mies was displaced by the psychological. It finds its own cultural sphere as negotiated space at the edge of critique. Postmodernism is purposely blind to its own situation. It saw instability, incited debate, removed temptations, agonies, and commitments to a present reality. There was nothing around to stand on but modernity. The postmodern emptied cities of the energy to produce great classical works, making for less to bring along in the movement into magnificent new buildings.

CHAPTER SEVENTEEN

Video Incest

Dese are de conditions dat prevail
— Jimmy Durante

Deep in mental space, there is a place of the imagination, a cool enveloping stillness the human mind seeks out. Distance covered in getting there is unknown. The destination is somewhere on the other side of language, as if before words. There, all is placid and pure. One stop ahead of Nirvana—where everyone has to get off—this place is more like a non-verbal clearing to visit once given the chance. Afterward, the visitor looks forward to returning.

Sufi mystic poet Rumi, founder of the ecstatic dancing order known in the West as Whirling Dervishes, once mused to no one in particular, "Out beyond ideas of wrong-doing and right-doing / There is a meadow, I will meet you there." Such ruminations are among the oldest reflective thought. From time to time, a new medium appears, a luminous and inviting way to get to the meadow, and the visitor is transported.

As with all things mental, eventually each state must be named. One twentieth-century state of universal possibility has been named *television*. It is a quiet and emergent steady state. This gazing that insulates also encourages the observer to assume there is something taking place, something unrelated to the medium, something valuable and lasting. Through its spectacular visual shadings and images, it is convincing as a self-generating historical moment. The television screen is used to screen-out as well as screen-in.

Watchers slip into the safety of underground secrets and watch, detached, while the camera actually looks at their stuff. This is privacy at the hearth of cool fires. Watchers can't be sure whether they are going to the meadow or have gone over to the medium. Many have suggested America takes place on, and in front of, the television.

Watchers continue to believe that words and pictures can have great power when used together in particular ways. White and black magic are based on appearance, or the "icon," and each requires a context of conventional belief. Like all icons, television also stops us and presents an impervious picture. Watchers are present to excitement once-removed. Through three million dots per second, television has moved viewers from the woodcut to the wave, and from the picture—which delights, provokes, or informs—to the icon of the century that *involves*. On the way to exploiting the unconscious, television became the reference for images of the ideal.

In its technology and intent, television is fragmentary. Its fluid nature makes it seem cool and smooth and universal. Programming on television has always come from a perspective of primal innocence that left room for disjointed ideals and private dreams. In recent decades it visualized goals for all Americans, a phenomenon Marshall McLuhan called, "keeping upset with the Joneses." If it showed confusing and contradictory ideas, it always gave out the antidote in the form of a clear prescription for how to think, behave, and live. Preferring the more sublime illusions of print, uneasy intellectuals took note of "educational television" broadcast stations. This oxymoron at least gave hope that evangelical advertising might ultimately be balanced with a drier discursive approach that would be less universal but correspondingly more ethical.

The action of television takes place beneath the surface. More than mere curiosity but less than a physical principle, television is a surface on which the viewer imprints his or her thought. Nothing is actually received as it is broadcast. The transaction is complete only with the interpretive cooperation of each member of the audience. In this sense, television is *thought displayed*. It is not random or even popular thought. Instead, it's a way of seeing secret thought, and for most of its history it has been displaying private thoughts. Through the screened facade, it takes charge then takes a viewer along, gliding over vast distances of cool excitement to periodic cadences of surprise and sudden epiphanies.

Unpredictable and often pleasantly strange, television is a phenomenon that creates the novel coinage of "hyper-intimacy." Clever social analysts characterize the impression of television as glorifying what is missing rather than what is in front of us. Soon, they say, we simply stop looking for absences. The effect television has upon viewers is a serious subject for those who have had little enough exposure to it to have retained a sort of *belle epoque* faculty of reason. For the rest, the effect of television is summed up in saying it robs one of the abstract.

The mistake was listening to those concrete thinkers who spawned the medium. These thinkers suggested that television was something more than a dazzling amusement and magic diversion. Drunken visions of television as technology able to produce, decode, and distribute truth inexpensively have begun to seem quite silly. All that television is capable of doing is displayed for the viewer. What is left out is her secret.

Some have suggested that the prime force behind television is tension. The history of television begins with the unbearable tension between black and white. These were the irresolute shades of television's infancy. Television grew up to be colored. Colors can dissipate tension. The power that keeps color and even black and white images coming is the eerie presence that deems this a cool medium.

Advancing cultures consumed with keeping track of their progress insist people cannot ignore the meaning of their experience, no matter how hard it may be to find. The idea of popular meaning has been reinforced by television as a way for everyone to agree life is meaningful and all could see how. Television became a passive medium, promoting concepts appropriated from the everyday. Something like group hallucination, it is beyond ordinary language, and a popular thing it is. Seeing success in promoting objects through extraordinary language, television has taken credit for delivering poetic imagination in a digestible format.

As device, television fits the popular notion of metaphor. Not only does television generate a plausible metaphor for understanding, it also feeds on metaphor for its material content. In mundane details it finds some approximation of thought, then displays nature metaphorically. Language, however, is necessary to point the viewer toward promoted meaning. Viewers cannot be trusted to get there alone. Metaphor in television is always incomplete and unsatisfying.

The biggest problem is meaning. Television learned to resolve its conflict between the need to trade in metaphor and its inability to complete the communication. The solution was imputing human qualities to virtually *everything* it promotes. Serious makers of metaphor call this "metonymy": things referring to other things to which they are somehow related. Objects take on the qualities, attributes, debts, fantasies, and dread of persons who possess them or who would like to:

> *The bouillabaisse at Table 6 wants her check.*
> *Our oboe is hungover again.*
> *The Post is in the lobby and needs a statement.*

The television must have been turned on when the metaphor-makers talked with the rhetoricians and came up with a special case of metonymy, that is, "synecdoche." This device identifies the whole by naming only a part:

> *He left his wheels at home.*
> *They did six fractures in Emergency before the chest came in.*
> *The sneaker has taken over Old Town.*

Metaphor essentially is the use of one thing to conceive of another and it's so much better when the meaning is understood. Original concepts of metaphor get lost in the derivative nature of possessing multiple synecdoches on top of too many metonymies. References become too far removed to be meaningful; the metaphorical machine breaks down and collapses. Meaning comes from the union of viewer with something very like herself. Television sits there, a visual medium of unspoken universal recognition, offering no clue to meaning but encouraging assent, acquiescence, and agreement. Aware of what it is people want to know, television puts hyper-intimacy in front of viewers to be absorbed and possessed over and over again.

A televised image was first delivered without the use of a visible connection by Philo T. Farnesworth, two years before the stock market crashed. Profit quickly became a necessary condition for television. What has emerged as "public television," as distinct from the more private urgings merchants push through the business end of distribution channels, has for obvious reasons embraced the same model. Public broadcasting must garner enormous sums to satisfy the appetite of a huge production apparatus. It builds marvelous empires that promote meaningful experience on the promise of ranging over the globe and into the mind. Public television has managed to produce, tape, and exhibit stage plays. It puts on concerts heard during simulated tours of galleries filled with masterworks. It has created a new medium that transliterates summaries of popular, yet enlightened, personal interpretations of meaningful experience. It has accomplished even more.

At its best, public (read *educational*) television succeeds in approximating pleasure. The hard lesson learned was that consistently producing excellent programming demands a guaranteed, usually exorbitant, budget. Facing these pressures, public television nonetheless was able to remain non-commercial until the 1980s.

There are limits to the utility of transmitting images around the world. If Marshall McLuhan can be trusted, we are in the midst of a post-literate return to tribal methods of learning: distilling meaning from personal experience using our own eyes and ears. Books are all used up. Abstract thinking evaporates. Neither refined nor subtle, television continues to shock and startle for profit. It uses the sound stage and animation to produce prime time prostitution, vengeance, mayhem, popular infidelity, and other delights that used to be taboo before secrets went on the air. Television makes any aberration appear normal through its *look*. This is a curious sleight-of-hand. No one is sure what to make of it.

Part of the television conspiracy, and there's no use production teams denying it, is that some people make a comfortable living in *television criticism*. If, as has been widely suggested, watchers of television have no interest in reading what is written about it, then television criticism must serve those who claim *not* to own a television, or at least not to watch it, even if someone else in the household brought one home and turned it on. This is an inexpensive index to good taste and a sign of breeding among the book-reading classes. Avoiding television has kept these citizens vibrant, engaging, well-informed, and happy. They always try to demonstrate all these qualities.

Television antagonists submit that it is all anodyne and cheap acculturation. Non-viewers are able to find enough drama in their lives without having to view someone else's. Even so, it is helpful to have professional critics to back them up so reliably in words they can read and understand. Critics, for their part, love to have readers, and it turns out that college students (who are usually fair readers) can watch only so much of anything, television included.

Watchers of television are less befuddled and more content with programming that is not only informational but well within television's capabilities to do well: *The Video Druid News* or *Opinions from Another Planet*.

Contemporary images are frequently too powerful to witness. Television is without conscience. This fixed-gaze persistence is taken by some for a brand of objectivity, and such objectivity amounts to truth. In a dark world, excited electrons display themselves for each other while the viewer observes through the looking glass. The viewer is stationary—television moves through him in cool equivalence. He thinks *he* is moving. Its odd qualities allow television to project and reflect, but it can also ingest. It works best—that is, most profitably—when nearly everything is in front of the eyes and almost nothing is behind them. In its domain, television runs to the wrong collaborator and takes the incestuous partner.

Television's essential hypnotics of liberation are what make television criticism such hard work. Its history is fragmentary, and the concluding story line disintegrates into myriad facets that bedazzle. Collapse of form leads to the confession that television occurs where the screen intersects with desire. But it draws only on itself, pretending it is the viewer, who pretends it's not. Variously dressed up as states of mind, television is literally exploded visions. These explosions instantly became public representations of one thing or another, and it is a tribute to its genius for survival that television has (for ninety years and more) maintained the spectacle and resisted moving through it.

Television runs special risks regarding obscenity and must ensure the viewer has something to look at and not into. Certain defenders of free speech stir their stumps and object to the term "television obscenity." They may have a point. How much imagination must they employ—how disciplined must the intellect be to produce a personal state of ecstasy from the anatomical picture?

In the end, television is not a human form. It alienates the historical mind and disables potent capacities. Yet it is virtuous, in that television has beauty, and could have more. Television is simplicity. It is valuable for looking at *where* life is happening, if not at *what*. As long as people understand how they are enjoying themselves, television can take them along. Television gives the illusion of polysemy, but it does not really offer many whirling meanings. It is only an *ordinary* dervish.

The final open secret is that television is American. Everything on television is in some way American or carries its objects through an American prism. Only America gets on TV. "Right-doing and wrong-doing," and where viewers go with it, usually is not fit for public display.

CHAPTER EIGHTEEN

Twisted Fate

This was a pretty country you took away from us.
— Quanah Parker

Passing from this world to whatever comes next is a natural thing. Still, it must be done with style. There are many styles, for everybody seems to be doing it eventually. Style rests in the manner of departing, either taking great pains and thought to prepare, or appearing to pay it no mind. It is human to suppose the voyager must have some sort of vision in order to master the unfamiliar distances. For those who remain behind, there is an empty sense that nothing really has moved but all of a sudden there somehow is a little more space.

Faced with the vast unknown, we naturally look to those special ones among us, the very few who are with us today who also see ahead—the ones who know things. Many native peoples of the five hundred nations saw us all as moving toward something great, so they sought out those who were able to make great things small and understandable. Great things need to be made small enough for our own field of vision. No matter the style, understanding great things is a rare gift that needs to be shared. The ones who know have an ability to compress everything into a single lifetime. They talk not about what lies beyond, rather what is here already. They connect the beyond with what lies within.

Uneasiness and difficulty are always part of the great visions. Yet there is universal appeal to them; many strange styles have carried us through the centuries. One is dealing, after all, with intellect and common emotion. Only questions of the spirit carry through. Taken together, these questions produce the best possible argument against being hopelessly resigned to fate.

Often, this is called "ethics," meaning behavior or conduct, as distinct from thought. It is common to see social and ethical problems manifest in our perpetual imbalance and confusion. Some modern figures emphasize that society is founded on how we handle essential human challenges: mental illness, crime and punishment, suffering of children, violence, care of the self. Such a list brings to mind a number of modern ethical thinkers, from Hindu Gandhi to French-Catholic Foucault. Crucial though these ethical perplexities may be, they do not tell us what we want. They are neither the lasting questions of the spirit, nor connected to a penetrating vision.

The language of vision is myth and symbolism. For native peoples, the questions of the spirit have been centered away from either temptation or redemption. They assume we are all in motion toward something great. The task is to blend, to preserve, to accept—a task for the here and the hereafter. Braided American ancestry includes the idea that Nature holds the secret of the beginning of time and as long as we are on and of the land, we are in perpetual holiness. There is nothing in this analogous to temptation.

Fusion of ancient and high cultures appears to have the effect on Western societies of coming together in abstract expressions that complicate everything. Americans possess a unique hollow within that forces us to reach back to separate origins. One is the primal spirit of native peoples. The other is the pre-renaissance attitude that existed in Europe before museums of the eighteenth and nineteenth century changed our connection with spirit. Navajo sand painting and the Book of Kells are separate, transcendent expressions from the ninth century. Europeans saw this continent as a spiritual terra incognita while the best part of native belief was not thinking much about the afterlife but trying to treat this place as though it is heaven.

American regenerative energy comes at the horizon. It is in the West. During the Depression, with its own confusion about progress and prosperity, the story of Black Elk's vision became known in the cities, and more important, perhaps to young native peoples. He was a holy man who expressed universal humanity during the decades of the great Messianic dream of desperate native nations, the "ghost dance" (expressing the belief that white people could be driven away and the traditional way of life restored), and the final massacre at Wounded Knee. He was the fourth generation in the Lakota to be called Black Elk. He was cousin to Crazy Horse. His great vision became his purpose. He understood it to be the story of all life, of the two-leggeds sharing the good of the earth with the four-leggeds—all part of spirit.

In May 1931, after due preparation, Black Elk smoked the pipe together with a small group, and he spoke to his trusted friend, John Neihardt, about his life and the Oglala Sioux:

In a fantastic landscape of mountains, rimmed, like a ruching, with color shooting upward to heaven, his vision came in pulses, like curtains of lightening. Suddenly standing on the high point, he saw the spiritual shapes of all things in one spirit, the sacred hoop of the Lakota engulfing day and night. At its center stood a flowering tree, to protect the children.

Most now think of his vision as allegory. It says to never act in a way undeserving of our better nature. The mountain he stood on in his vision is known as the Black Hills, "but anywhere is the center of the world," Black Elk added in the manner of a Zen master. When he was a young boy, Black Elk heard the words of an old vision, one from long before the coming of the *wasichus* (a term that designated white men but without referring to color): "You shall live in square gray houses in a barren land, and…shall starve." Later, he lived through the bleak prophesy of his grandfathers.

Visions in North America were drawn on tribal archetypes: the cardinal points—Sky and Earth. The importance of Black Elk's vision is its fusion of particular and universal elements that come to us all in our personal frailty and lone isolation. Spiritual power of the vision requires it be shared with others. It is of little use to the recipient alone, coming too late—as it does—after his own twisted fate.

Dreams of knowing arrive unsolicited. Sometimes the tribe looks to one who can dream for all—the Pueblo shaman, the Hopi sorcerer. The tradition of the Zuni is to huddle together under a pantheon of totems as life unfolds. Visionary experience is not predicted and can be only partly communicated. Confronted by a flaming rainbow encircling the earth, Black Elk understood more than he saw.

The late 1800s were hurried and modern times. Geography in America shifted. The same year Black Elk was born, 1863, a treaty was put before the lower Nez Perce Indians of the Grande Ronde. They declined to sign it. Later, under their remarkable young leader, Chief Joseph, they would endure many seasons of watching their beautiful valleys fill up with industrious settlers. Joseph saw himself as diplomat, representing both the families and the Dreamers. These were the old ones, who preserved the doctrine of a complete Earth. The complete Earth was in no need of man's cultivation or other disturbance. Nez Perce had been most hospitable to Captain Meriwether Lewis, Lieutenant William Clark, and the Corps of Discovery expedition generations before, and Joseph recalled the vow of his grandfathers to always stay at peace with the United States.

Rather than retire to the reservation, the non-treaty Nez Perce insisted they had never traded their land. The Earth is one body, they said, and they could never give any part of it over. However, their chief rallied them with the natural resources of his mind, and rather than fight, he led the men, women, and babies out of reach of the army's long rifles. Practicing the art of peace, he avoided conflict and capture. With energy and endurance, Joseph was living Jeffersonian principles of many generations.

For many years, Joseph had held in his heart things the white man had said. When will the white man learn to speak the truth?

Nearly a hundred years later, Bob Dylan gave his first New York concert. He came from North Dakota Territory. He offered up truth in his personal premonitions. A generation became aware of the problems of misplaced integrity. More recently, the Nobel Committee has looked back at Dylan as one who knows things.

Dylan has reached back a century and seen that treatment of native peoples ruined any shot Americans had at redemption. He also noticed that at about the same time, 1871, poet Arthur Rimbaud had expressed a certain conviction in a letter: "The poet makes himself seer by a long, prodigious and rational disordering of the senses."

Bob Dylan appears as an *eminence noir*, seeing the American habit and making it metaphor. His spiritual ancestors include Blake, Whitman, and Ginsberg—but his significance for the fourth and fifth generations removed from Black Elk is that Dylan has been among us. He tells of the other side of vision, a place for the dispossessed of the universe. According to the Dylan catechism, the three temptations are ego states of confusion: ambition, guilt, desire.

In his collected works, Dylan lays down the righteous and deplorable in American custom and waits for us to learn the difference. Americans have to be busy doing something, and that's part of everyone's dilemma. Better selves are always nearby, and that's what gives such bleak horror to other parts of Dylan's vision. His interest and attention are on puzzling out the wrongheadedness of our rules, as with his "My Back Pages":

> *"Equality," I spoke the word*
> *As if a wedding vow.*
> *Ah, but I was so much older then*
> *I'm younger than that now*

Chief Joseph returns to us standing quietly through Dylan's evocation in "Shelter from the Storm"—

> *I was burned out from exhaustion, buried in the hail*
> *Poisoned in the bushes an' blown out on the trail*

After his vision, Black Elk was *brought back to life*. Like all visionaries, he knew more than he had been shown, and he was shown more than he could tell. Whether this land is yours and Woody Guthrie's or not, it has, for some time been a place where people stood on the hill, looked westward, and surveyed their prospects. Children of white Europeans felt they were earning a continent, marching to destiny from Cahokia to the Shoshone in Oregon.

In the latter twentieth century, Dylan offered up unique clarity. He repeated that the wanderings of a quest misdirected lead to anxiety, mourning the mystical experience of our better selves. He reminds us of universal melody, though he probably is not, as some burnt out heads have suggested, the songwriter of the century. There are, after all—Irving Berlin, George Gershwin, Jerome Kern. Cole Porter also had something going on. No other, though, has written like

Dylan—no one has put himself in the midst of an American moral vision of what we should have been—well, maybe Harold Arlen.

It is popular now to look to native peoples for a true map that shows a better route to a penetrating vision. There is inviting poetry in the sensibilities of the Mandan and Shoshone, who, for example, called the mirror shown them by Lewis and Clark, "solid water."

There has always been variety in America. Lakota produced Black Elk but also raised ancient chiefs who fought brutally with their brothers long before *wasichus* arrived. Out of their own arrogance, many had the bad habit of humiliating their peaceful neighbors. Notwithstanding all these disagreeable truths, the path to American vision has led through Native Territory.

In the aftermath of flight, Chief Joseph asked only for a small piece of land in the valley of his people, and that they be provided with a teacher for the children. When the great chief died at age sixty-four, the doctor attending him reported the cause of death as a broken heart.

Looking back from the high hill of old age, Black Elk said he could see the butchered women and children lying heaped and scattered in the hard rain and crimson mud—like the broken hoop of his vision. Soon, the mud was buried in the blizzard. A single dream, the same dream to many peoples of the land, had died. *It was a beautiful dream.*

Motion toward great things continues. Visionaries reassure the rest that all know things that cannot be taught. If great things are bound to return, then all are fulfilled in one spirit—anonymous, tiny, but complete. Perhaps the white man invented redemption, for he was most in need of it. He twisted his fate with that of others and he closed it out. Dylan reminds us again, in "With God on Our Side":

The cavalries charged
The Indians died
Oh the country was young
With God on its side

All of a sudden, there somehow is a little more space.

CHAPTER NINETEEN

Bert Lonestone, Left Field

Baseball is ninety percent mental. The other half is physical.
— Yogi Berra

Several minutes with a scorecard should convince anyone that playing the game is only part of it. Thinking about playing the game takes up far more time. Players and entourage alike devote years to its mysteries. In practice, the game itself takes up some finite period. It opens, it rumbles through the middle innings, and it's over. Nearly every game ever started has, by now, ended. Some number of them are still going on. Others are, of course, about to start. Taken together with anticipation of the game and reminiscences of the game, the game accounts for just about all of recent time.

American optimism invented the game and is renewed annually by it. From the very beginning, the top of the first first, its ethereal nature has been recognized. Each event of the game has been recorded, down to its quantum unit. Data are compiled and analyzed again and again by each successive generation of scholars and theorists. Nothing new is sought or expected. In fact, it is the soul of affirmation that nothing is ever found to be at odds with the original design.

In its statistics, patterns are noticed. The game knows these as *streaks*. They shoot by, on the curve of space. The scorecard keeps the record.

Long before even the National League, native peoples played an ancient game French Canadians later adapted and named *lacrosse*. The pure, original form of lacrosse went on continuously and covered great distances. Some believed it never stopped, instead having active and quiescent stretches. Players picked up their sticks and attacked for a while, then the action subsided. It could go on this way for years.

The American game is *baseball*. It, too, goes on continuously. In back alleys and front yards, players stretch, collect their gloves and bats, check the bases, and look around to see who showed up to play for the other side. Someone chooses the best-looking for the game ball, unless he is going to pitch. Then, the National Anthem sounds, or at least the six notes of its final cadence echo through the mind.

Controlled tension that rises and falls, like a throw from the outfield, makes the game therapeutic. Treatment is prescribed every day, weather permitting—vitamins for the psyche and a balm for the limbs. The game has a dual nature that, rather than being perplexing, is a comfort. As ideal abstraction, it vibrates sympathetically within. But it also creates an absolute world, providing hope and refuge in the immutable force of its rules. Only the game can ignore dimensions that constrain our physical universe. Look it up.

Rules structure the game. Pleasures derive from the abundance of situations that can occur within the rules. There are neither too many rules, nor too few; the number of rules is absolutely adequate. Circumstances are described with cardinal precision and are beyond appeal: the score, runs in, runners on, the lead, the sign, the count.

Batting, base running, and throwing are *fundamental* to the game. Theorists stop there and claim everything else is derivative. Players know better. Fundamentals include the slide, the tag, hitting the cutoff man, backing up the play, putting the bat on the ball for the squeeze, and maybe chewing something. Coaches say it's fundamental to avoid giving up the Big Inning. Fans know from experience the fundamental importance of argument. The game allows for argument and sets down its rules. Baseball is a human activity; argument, therefore, is encouraged.

In matters of law, the standard applied is "agreeable to reason and sound judgment." By contrast, rules in the game are absolute and are reinforced, more or less intelligibly, by the oracle of the game, the umpire. For any situation, there is a single response that is the correct action. Other actions may be permitted—they may get you out of the inning—but they are not the one correct response. Only one act fits. There is never interpretation, only the final word, and it is absolute. A player must therefore recognize each situation as being, in essence, *basic*. Then he must execute the correct action. Outside the park, relationships of things in motion are governed by dynamic influences. Inside the game, it's absolute fundamentals.

Baseball recapitulates the universe on principles that used to be, well, fundamental. Fundamental actions of the game extend through timeless physical dimensions of space in which the third baseman scoops up a grounder and rifles the ball to an empty spot, knowing baseball's terrestrial mechanics require that the first baseman will materialize and glove it. Since the first pitch, more than a century-and-a-half ago, the game has remained absolute in its Newtonian character. Meanwhile, the world outside the park changed.

The twentieth century began with a very Big Inning. Physicists batted around in the order. Every time they asked Nature something about atomic structure, they got a paradoxical answer. The mechanistic universe of the Cartesian view that Newton liked so well seemed not to be the case. No longer conceived of as a machine of multitudinous parts, the universe was pictured as indivisible, composed of interrelated objects in unfathomable space, understood only in terms of cosmic patterns. The record book was open to interpretation. If knowledge of the universe was indeed relative, there could be no use for fundamentals. That meant no errors. Newton was thrown out, and the side was retired.

Astronomers limit what they call our "horizon" to something like fourteen billion years. This, they say, represents the time light has had to travel. They suggest our universe is finite but unbounded and, although physics is no longer absolute, there now are choices in how to interpret it.

One choice is *quantum theory*. This says the world is unpredictable. Worse yet, anything science measured changes—not just our understanding of it, but it changes what is being measured. Nothing can be determined with accuracy, and it gets no better with practice. Meaning, if that's what everyone is after, is derived only from relationships, and nothing is independent of the spectator. In the modern quantum universe, evidence that there is gravity is more important than gravity. None of this makes a pop fly coming out of the sun any easier to handle.

Another choice, *chaos theory*, is no better for the game. Its major concern is how nonlinear systems adapt to the world over time. Positive and negative actions set up situations; stability and instability play together in what is seen as randomness within constraints. Constraints may be described, even predicted, but not the outcome. Chaos theory says the world is knowable but we'll never get there, due to the extreme sensitivity of the original conditions and the importance of small—that is, *really* small—differences. Information fundamental to knowing flows across space and time in innumerable guises and dynamic states. A streaking liner becomes an improbable notion in the chaos, and it may go undetected.

If there were two enduring human concepts to come out of the nineteenth century, and one of them is baseball, even Americans would have to admit the other is probably electromagnetism. At some time before the World Series of 1905, a young physicist who had been given his unconditional release by Swiss Polytechnic, came out of left field to propose that the speed of light was fixed. This gave the game a boost. Speed, he reiterated, is a measure of distance over some unit time. If the speed of light is a physical constant, then the flow of time must change. The rate at which time passes is conditional, as any pitcher with his good stuff knows. Relatively speaking, this was indeed a special theory.

Fundamentals Newton played by were not considered arbitrary, just conditioned by the nature of observation. Furthermore, there is a general principle that governs both infield and outfield. It says there is an equivalence between gravity and acceleration that determines the path of anything coming off the hitter's bat. In the universe, gravity comes vacuum-packed, but in the field matter and energy shape the effect of gravity, and that determines whether a hit goes for extra bases.

Baseball lives on statistics, so an analyst can have a strong effect on the game, particularly if that analyst looks for necessary connections. Imagine the manager yelling to his pensive young left fielder standing quietly at the fence,

> "Hey, what's the matter in the field?"
>
> "Hmm," thinks the player, staring quizzically over toward right. "It's true, matter is important. Every gram of it contains vast energy… no doubt some factored constant applied to the matter itself…but he's right, it must be the field that accounts for almost everything. The ball's motion is not uniform, it has an initial motion, then the force of the field acts upon that motion, then there is the final motion. At some point, inevitably, every fungo begins to fall."

The young fielder finds that the concept of a vector helps him anticipate the inevitable course of the sphere that lands dead at his feet. But for the manager, these distractions have broken his fielder's concentration, and it means the player will need a crisp vector to home plate when he should have recognized the basic situation as a routine fly ball.

Point of observation clearly matters. The game is based on straight lines. It always seeks the unobstructed view (say, halfway up the line on the third base side). Lines of force, on the other hand, are constructed in the field where there is essentially no matter present. By the late innings, our left fielder understands the question, what's the matter in the field? He spits, then answers, "Not much."

A sort of weightless vertigo comes with this concept of the field—the single most important construction of the mind since Newton's time. The game resists imagination, so it's not easy to realize that it's not charges and particles but the field, the space between everything, that is essential. What is called *matter* is simply a great concentration of field energy in a small space.

Matter impresses the senses as solid mass within the field. The ball is its own changing field, the point of greatest intensity traveling from the plate with a velocity equal to the ball itself. The field is everything and the only reality. According to field theory, at bats probably don't count.

Of course, science is a creation of the human mind; its free ideas and concepts are meant to connect with an emerging picture of reality. For those who claim the game is divinely inspired, this separates science from baseball. They believe the most primitive idea of all, namely, the object. The object is tied up with statistics to create an advanced concept that is at least on par with science. Every speedster at short acquires insight of space-time and sees that the game's description of the real world is anchored in the statistical record.

The general theory of relativity created problems in the field. It said all space between the bags and outside the foul lines has geometric properties determined by matter. Exceedingly small bits of matter exert nearly all the influence. Compressing all particles in the universe, removing all space between them in the fashion of a *big crunch*, reduces all matter to something the size of a baseball. It becomes evident that *everything* is in the field. Everybody's an outfielder.

The conclusion from left field was that the universe is finite but unbounded. Closed spaces without limits it seemed *are* conceivable. Furthermore, light is special, and not just to see the change up coming. If light's speed is constant, it makes incomprehensible yet finite distances acceptable in the changing flow of time.

On its face, the game might seem to oppose the notion of relativity. Left fielders are not usually taken seriously, particularly if they can't handle a slider despite understanding that it's traveling in multiple planes simultaneously. In baseball, there are no acts of revision. The game requires sacrifice and reassures with its own constants. Sometimes the player must "give himself up with the bunt." Yet as if in consolation, he knows he needs to always "hit the cripple" when it's three-and-one. Baseball plays with time in its own way, even inventing a new time: it makes *twi-nighter* a natural idea.

Between games there is space and time. In the field, space-time appears tranquil, uniform, and wound to a bygone standard—its own tension gradually relaxing to a comfortable tempo, only to be punctuated by cataclysmic events. Pressure is relieved by the player's reflex, connected to instinct. Explosions of events, baseball novas, are never completely unpredictable. There is always a clairvoyant who has seen just beforehand the single, correct reflex that exists in the very next moment.

America's game is not concerned with reconciliation or compromise and has no truck with syncretistic science. The phenomenon that perhaps best illustrates baseball's absolute nature is its own invention. It is efficiency in the presence of the force. It is a calculus that takes place in the center of the field. Turning the *double play* is in no sense relative. Rather, the infield fixes on the point of convergence at the keystone, second base. Players work to reduce and perfect their complementary motion in the beatific simplicity of a single closed curve of energy. Only fundamentals apply. Practice makes it inevitable. Done in a flash of predictable yet startling intensity, light carries the image of the double play to the spectator. For an instant, time has somehow slowed down. The double play is an expression of minimizing effort, eliminating extraneous movement, redirecting energy along one instinctive reflex. It is a ringed ballet, indifferent to the runners. Objects move through the point of convergence in a fluid plasma state. Time is not part of doubling them up.

Parks are the spaces that preserve the absolute character of the game. Inside parks, the Newtonian primary colors of yellow sun and blue sky mix to produce the emerald field. The players' bleed red. Between games, there appears to be nothing: a bleached vacuum where time may be passing, but no one can say for sure. What is often witnessed in modern stadiums and huge domes is spectacle. The game is played in parks. In an empty park, the player that lives inside every fan stands motionless, recollecting past games pulled gently into consciousness. Like imagined universes smaller than an atom, they are playing through the innings in a mote of dust in a morning sunbeam.

All science wants is a picture of reality as a closed system that is comprehensible. The ballpark is a useful principle:

finite space yet no limits. Inside, it is both fluid and mechanistic; absolute in its dimensions: a 95-foot radius from the pitcher's rubber, a 90-foot diamond, 127 feet across at the transept, a 26-foot batting circle, 60 feet 6 inches from mound to plate, a 6-foot base path, 60 feet from the catcher's spikes to the backstop, 410 feet to straight-away dead center. Yet it is relative in its speed.

"Baseball field theory" is based on the idea of what's coming. It holds the ideal close and gives physicists a platform for the imagination to explore a true reality. The game teaches awareness, continuity, and the persistence of the absolute. A voice from left field reminded everyone that change is measured against something constant, some phenomenon that doesn't change. No one expects to attain the ideal. In fact, it's assumed it never will be. Ask which we are likely to see first—travel approaching the speed of light or a Red Sox-Cubs World Series?

The game is America's national thought experiment in four-dimensional space-time. Relativity applies to the game precisely for what it teaches. Its conditions obtain only within the foul lines, where time is suspended. From his unique position of observation, slightly red-shifted in left field, a lone theoretical physicist concluded that quantum theory may have set real limits on his own idea of the unified field. Two different realities, gravitational ether and electromagnetism, seemed to him to require a new understanding that would combine the ball and the field in one structure. As the innings rumble along, there is enticing confusion at each new thought. Yet the concept of order must somehow be over the fence, out of sight but universal. Some days you win, some days you lose, some days it rains.

A week after Opening Day, 1955, the vectors out of left field stopped. The left fielder's last thought was about faith in the harmony of the park, the moment, the universe. In its absolute proportions, the game demonstrates the immutable truth of his insight—that the center of the universe is relative. For some, it's second base, for others it's the bottom of the fourth. For the slugger, it's Louisville. Optimism and renewal exist in indeterminate time at some point in curved space—but it's only a game in a field.

CHAPTER TWENTY

Mei Kuo

Please don't shoot the piano player. He is doing his best.
— Anonymous

When pressed to declare the American moment of any century, most readily will say it is *liberty*. Liberty is the whole design for a lived sense of the eternal. A peculiar egalitarianism has evolved here. It was present in some recognizable form long before the arrival of Europeans or Africans. The result has been living in the extended present. Men and women are spiritual in relating to the world, and since pre-history America has, in its innumerable ages and cultures, not just allowed for but encouraged the continuous presence of spirit. Ritual has been optional. Dress has always been casual.

If there is an American philosophy, it is surely rooted in liberty and the land, viewed in the forever. Habit is bound up in this geography of virtue that grants to the mind the ordinary joyful flow of undirected thought. Perhaps this is what makes liberty most valuable. Ironically, the moral lesson that one cannot profit from the labor of another against his or her will has been hard-learned.

Nowhere is there a better case for pragmatism than in America—no better argument for the logic of change. As a Republic, America was conceived as a noble work of the progressive will. It remains a place of promise, presumption, ineffable purpose, and divine providence. An earthly realm of prospect, it makes all wealthy who believe in the possibility of collective desire.

Yet elder societies view with dismay the modern version of full-dollar capitalism, as though it were a dysfunctional circus, too fantastic to ignore. Grant that capitalism practiced in a societal context appears to be substantially different than capitalism predicated on the gospel of the individual. Hence, it must be conceded that it has failed the society of the Republic in—for example—health, education, and the general welfare. Nevertheless, there is the persistent ring of individual purpose, each one employing liberty to invent a spiritual life and personal destiny.

What, then, is the common dream of all modern American self-stylists? The capitalist who exploits freedom though cares little for liberty, proclaims, "an American is one who deserves more than he has." But the enduring Spirit of Liberty, deftly playing capitalism as metaphor for the left hand, urges, "an American is one who is becoming more than she is."

One becomes American by being received into the broad lap of the land. From dim Europe ancient peoples came, leaving behind them both mindless prejudice and good manners. For the last four hundred years, they have melted into a new race. Here, labor is based on the natural principle of enlightened self-interest, giving the appearance of a frolicsome jaunt through industry, a playground of production.

It is worth acknowledging that, although purpose is essential to the American character, there exists no collective purpose, for America has always lacked the necessary conditions of either a homogeneity of thought or an authoritarian dictum of taste. An American must entertain new ideas and form opinions, practical and preposterous.

How troubling then to acknowledge that war has worked well for this country. Such darkness of character is better recognized by the rest of the world. The world notices American blindness, bluster, and waste. Peace and equality, however, are truly hard to find anywhere, and their renewal as American grail more recently has become a common quest in Europe and beyond.

French-American J. Hector St. John de Crèvecoeur, in his *Letters from an American Farmer*, urged eighteenth-century Americans that they ought to love this country and its exuberant fields much more than that of their fathers. It is probably true that here one stops being Norwegian, or Greek, or Korean, and becomes someone with a first name holding the secular American hymnal under the left arm, leaving the right hand free for a handshake.

From its beginning, America existed as an idea in a land farthest from it. In 1784, the Empress of China, first of the famous China clippers built by an enterprising group of New England capitalists, sailed up the Pearl River and anchored at Canton. A propitious event, it probably was not the first contact between America and the Celestial Empire. After all, tea dumped into Boston harbor more than a decade before very likely had been delivered through the East India Company's Chinese trading partners.

It was reported that the Emperor thought Americans barbaric, low, and worthy of his contempt—a general reaction the Son of Heaven held for all kingdoms to the south and east. Such is the record of esteemed geographer Wei Yuan's *Hai-kuo t'u-chih* of 1794 in the *Illustrated Treatise on the Sea Kingdoms*. Soon after, however, a legendary view of America was dreamed by Chinese who knew little or nothing of it.

Ethereal from the start, the unofficial Chinese story of America became more potent over the next hundred years. The further inland one journeyed, the more a vision of *mei kuo (beautiful kingdom)* was tucked in the minds of villagers of the valleys and mountains. For anyone's chance of seeing it, the legendary land might as well have been the moon.

Many Chinese, of course, did come in the late-nineteenth century, and they tell a different story. But for those who, in the early days, only heard tales of America, it seemed a place just beneath the divine.

With first contact between separate worlds, history often blends with myth. Early America was thought by some to hold the promise of dignity and a sense of joy. For the decades this legend endured, it grew powerful by its repetition. Received ideas and wishful thinking in China historically have grown to unique fullness through repetition by many: *China—The People's Republic of People.*

Since the Manchu Emperors moved into Peking in 1644, internal security has remained the major official program of successive Chinese governments. Much of the openness and creative beauty of Ming Dynasty China is missing, somehow absent from the modern day. Yet not even the Manchus had been able to protect what they saw as vital internal Chinese interests in states of the inner Asian frontier and the South China Sea. Nor could they halt foreign incursions.

America's arrival at Canton, having the full encouragement of President Washington, was of far greater interest and excitement to the visitor than the host. *Unofficial* China, however, is not easily reined in. Heaven, after all, was its own divine province long before Buddha—a place to put feelings stolen from living.

Americans had sailed through the straits of Enlightenment and were buoyed by Liberty's great moment. The American Republic as invention draws on the extravagant dreams of other nations. These dreams become the stuff of how Americans imagine themselves to be. Americans are busy; liberty is an active principle. Liberty is nearly a sufficient first principle—nearly, but not quite. The necessary corollary to liberty is avoiding the great danger. The danger many Americans sense is missing life's deep happiness.

In more lucid secular afternoons of undirected thought, Americans instinctively know this to be the common hazard; it is not that humans will make an absolute turd of life but that they will fall short of destiny. American hymnist Phillips Brooks put it this way: "(to be) unconscious of life ablaze ... and be content to have it so." Liberty does not concern itself with husks and trappings but is meant to remove any excuse for being satisfied with a life that falls short of its best. Everything counts.

Rome is frequently trotted out as an instructive illustration of almost anything, and it is evident the Roman

Republic at some point began to believe its own press. Its greatness was located in the minds of peoples who would never actually go there. The Fall of Rome, historians write, was the inevitable end to its decline—but it's not clear, to begin with, when it fell. History, myth, and legend are tangled briars overgrowing the column of truth. Placing the Fall is an exercise in *intended relevance* tempered with anxieties that circulate within the particular historian.

There is, as luck would have it, a date for the Fall of Rome. In fact, there is no end to dates. Many say it was all done with the sack of Rome by the gatecrashers of 410 CE. Others pin it on deposing the last Roman emperor in 476 CE. There are arguments for the reign of Constantine or Augustus in 31 BCE. Hannibal, it must be said, was remembered in this context by Toynbee, and the visit of Family Barci (by way of Barcelona) was in the third century BCE. A small but vocal group of bloodshot *ragazzi* insist that Rome only fell in the late twentieth century with the passing of Federico Fellini.

In a similar vein, there have been straight-faced conclusions as to the actual cause of the Fall of Rome. Historians have offered arguments for two hundred or more distinct causes. This attests to the basic problem with history as a scholarly profession based on statements of faith. The Fall of Rome is instructive, they say, but no one is sure why.

It is popular now to speak of the *decline of America*. The current decline, it is argued, is caused by inward destruction of the social experiment. The experiment has sought somehow to give order to liberty.

William James—American physician, thinker, and ringleader of pragmatism, used to upbraid his European counterparts by asking them to specify the *cash value* of a particular philosophical proposition. The wholesale lesson of America may be *perseverance*. America perseveres in its perpetual decline, opening up to mystery while pushing ahead toward dignity and joy.

The Chinese accepted the American reality at full value. As with Rome, the way in which others view great states changes the collected mythology. America has been repeatedly changed in this way by China. This actually covers the past fifteen thousand years, and is difficult to ignore. It has been demonstrated that Asians were the first inhabitants of America, having crossed the land bridge near the Arctic Circle. These were the ancestors of native peoples the early Spanish conquerors called *In Dios*. It is easier to understand extreme tensions in the idea of America when recalling that on the east coast, Vikings came ashore, but many years before in the west, it was forebears of Ch'ins and Hans.

In our own age, China again has served as a reminder of the American mythology. Chinese political speakers talk openly of admiration for Abraham Lincoln as an example of advancing human tolerance and social progress. There are always glaring contradictions, however. When Chinese students—not sojourners and traveling scholars but Chinese *students*—died in the streets of the capital for the democratic ideal, it was not the likeness of Buddha they rallied to, and certainly not that of Confucius.

Instead, they drew along with them the likeness of a century-old French interpretation of the American asylum: a rough-cast, thirty-foot replica of *Liberty*, as she stands in the harbor of New York. Young Chinese apparently are taken with the French idea of how Americans see themselves. America has trouble resisting it too, and so it is incorporated into the decline.

Liberty is not connected to the ethnic experience in America, except by way of neutralizing it. Ethnology of America we call "Americana." It is a wholly implausible term. Henry James (elder brother to William) said, "it's a complex fate, being an American." Emerson withdrew, offering an observation from his own ethnic experience that "to become American we go to Europe."

The underside of Americana is the obsession described by one of America's cold-eyed commentators, H.L. Mencken. He delivered the universal condemnation: "Every third American devotes himself to improving and uplifting his fellow-citizens, usually by force."

In the voyage to the headwaters of America's current decline, the traveler inevitably is tossed up on the jagged rocks of responsibility. Neither the swells of Americana nor the tides of Americanism, this drift is a pathological state that might be called "Amnerica." Amnerica manifests itself as a pre-senile condition characterized by the struggle for purpose—dementia brought on by remote memory lapse. Something important has evaporated from memory. Becalmed in amnerimonic latitudes, the traveler may recall what others have said about the Republic, thereby to correct the course. This is a blend of vanity and panic. Avatars of America have been misinterpreted. There is little help coming from observers. This sort of memory loss is resistant to reefer, and it can't be treated with cleaner drugs.

Mei kuo, it is now clear, is American legend and not Chinese. It is just a dream, but it is America's dream alone. It is true that some hopeful souls may accurately translate the words as "beautiful" country, but the Chinese convention in naming is phonetic: Mei 美丽 the convenient abbreviation for *Mei-li-Jian*, *Amer-i-ca*. The Mandarin phrase seeks only to bring the *sound* of the word into Chinese.

Deep in the provinces, America is now thought to be a place where one must stay in after dark or risk violent crime and death. Young Chinese continue in the same vein and cite similar examples. Mandarin for "Germany," *De Guo* 德国, repeats the first sound of *Deutschland*, adding *guo* (these days replacing the less-often used *kuo*). Students point out the irony in *De*. Its meaning, by itself, is "morality." This is not thought to be an apt description of Germany in the last century—*moral country!* They scoff, then they laugh. No one remembers Schiller or Goethe—only Goebbels.

Transliteration runs the risk of unintended meaning, so it's best to weigh received ideas carefully. America perseveres. The aim is still an uninterrupted apprehension of the best that space and time have to offer. How is one able to balance perfectly his or her polarities and paradoxes? Life occurs within a certain amplitude, and between cakewalk and cliff-hang there is only a faint impulse to correct for drift.

America has contrived a kind of air lock that contains all the reality it can stand emotionally. Call it a "peer pressure seal," it closes off the experiment in liberty in the name of self-preservation. The American resource is unique and requires every sort of courage to keep it up. But Americans need somehow to reconcile these things in life. Having walked on the moon of the mandarins and returned, how does this bring courage to the imagination?

The logic of change is all the security Americans are likely to get. An idea held in the mind was proof enough for Aristotle that the substance of that idea must exist—somewhere. Chinese phonetics produced the words for "beautiful country." Now it is left to American metaphysics to locate mei kuo, "in common hours," in Thoreau's phrase.

The American Century closed before the millennium. Sixty generations have increased the chances for each one to live a life imagined. It was a short century. If defined by world events, it stretched from the end of the First World War to the fall of European communism, totaling seventy-five years.

Perhaps living longer offers more hours to look back. Each millennial cusp of the Common Era is like a stepping stone, showing how the Western world was shaped first by Romans (1 CE), a thousand years later by Vikings, and a thousand years after that by Americans. We might wonder whether centuries to come will all be a bit shorter.

Chapter Epigraphs

CHAPTER ONE:
Life is something to do when you can't get to sleep. Fran Lebowitz, American writer and humorist (b. 1950).

CHAPTER TWO:
Whither goest thou, America, in thy shiny car in the night? Jack Kerouac, American novelist and poet of French-Canadian descent (1922-1969). "What is the meaning of this voyage to New York? What kind of sordid business are you on now? I mean, man, whither goest thou? Whither goest thou, America, in thy shiny car in the night?" *On the Road*, Part II, Chapter 3.

CHAPTER THREE:
The older I get, the more vivid is my recollection of things that never happened. Mark Twain [Samuel Langhorne Clemens], American author and humorist (1835-1910). *Autobiography.*

CHAPTER FOUR:
At first, I didn't know what to call it. Dizzy Gillespie, American jazz trumpeter, bandleader, and composer (1917-1993). Alyn Shipton, *Groovin' High—The Life of Dizzy Gillespie* (2001).

CHAPTER FIVE:
Somewhere between the gradual extinction of human liberty and the total extinction of terrestrial life.... Ursula K. LeGuin, American author (1929-2018). Introduction (added 1976) to *The Left Hand of Darkness* (1969).

CHAPTER SIX:
Guard well your spare moments. They are like uncut diamonds. Ralph Waldo Emerson, American essayist, lecturer, philosopher, and poet (1803-1882).

CHAPTER SEVEN:
And we are magic talking to itself, noisy and alone. Anne Sexton, American poet (1928-1974). *You, Doctor Martin.*

CHAPTER EIGHT:
It is easier to build strong children than to repair broken men. Frederick Douglass [Frederick Augustus Washington Bailey], American social reformer, abolitionist, orator, writer, statesman, and diplomat (1818-1895).

CHAPTER NINE:
Everywhere I go, I'm asked if I think the universities stifle writers. My opinion is that they don't stifle enough of them. Flannery O'Connor, American writer and essayist (1925-1964).

CHAPTER TEN:
Gertrude was always right. Ernest Hemingway, American author and journalist (1899-1961). "Gertrude [Stein] was always right," in conversation with John Peale Bishop and

quoted in Bishop's "Homage to Hemingway," *The New Republic* (11 November 1936).

CHAPTER ELEVEN:
Draw in your head and sleep the long way home. Hart Crane [Harold Hart Crane], American poet (1899-1932). "Draw in your head, alone and too tall here. / Your eyes already in the slant of drifting foam; / Your breath sealed by the ghosts I do not know; / Draw in your head and sleep the long way home." *Voyages, III.*

CHAPTER TWELVE:
All great art is born of the metropolis. Ezra Pound, expatriate American poet and critic (1885-1972). *The Selected Letters of Ezra Pound, 1907-1941.*

CHAPTER THIRTEEN:
Courage is the price that life exacts for granting peace. Amelia Earhart, American aviation pioneer and author (1897-1939). *Courage.*

CHAPTER FOURTEEN:
Our lives are merely strange dark interludes in the electrical display. Eugene O'Neill, Irish American playwright and Nobel Laureate (1888-1953). *Strange Interlude* (1928).

CHAPTER FIFTEEN:
I've seed de first en de last... I seed de beginning, en now I sees de endin. William Faulkner, American writer and Nobel Laureate (1897-1962). *The Sound and the Fury* (1929).

CHAPTER SIXTEEN:
I was a little disappointed on receiving your rather lengthy letter to find no mention of money. Groucho Marx [Julius Henry Marx], American comedian (1890-1977). Letter to Alistair Cooke (8 July 1957).

CHAPTER SEVENTEEN:
Dese are de conditions dat prevail. Jimmy Durante, American singer, pianist, comedian, and actor (1893-1980).

CHAPTER EIGHTEEN:
This was a pretty country you took away from us. Quanah Parker, Scots-Irish statesman, war leader of the Quahadi band of the Comanche Nation, and last Chief of the Comanche (1845-1911).

CHAPTER NINETEEN:
Baseball is ninety percent mental. The other half is physical. Yogi Berra [Lawrence Peter Berra], American major league baseball catcher, outfielder, and manager (1925-2015). Bill Adler, *Baseball Wit* (1986).

CHAPTER TWENTY:
Please don't shoot the pianist. He is doing his best. Anonymous. "Over the piano was printed a notice: *Please do not shoot the pianist. He is doing his best.*" Oscar Fingal O'Flahertie Wills Wilde, Irish poet and playwright (1854-1900). *Impressions of America: Leadville* (Leadville, Colorado, 1882).

Index

Achilles, 98
Adams, Abigail, 49
Adams, John, 49, 51–53
Adams, John Quincy, 52
Alfred of Britain, 4
American Shinto, 50
Anderson, Sherwood, 20
Anglicanism, 50
Aphrodite, 83
Aquinas, 54
Ariadne, 84
Aristotle, 185, 61, 68
Arjuna, 48, 54
Arlen, Harold, 163
Art Deco, 99
Aryans, 131
Aspasia, 84
Athena, 98
Atlas, 17
atmen, 76
Augustine, 54
automatic writing, 61
Aymara, 126
Bacon, Francis, 58
Baker, Chet, 122
Balkans, 51, 104
Barcelona Pavilion, 145
baseball field theory, 174
Basie, Count, 30
Baudelaire, Charles, 8, 38
Bauhaus, 144
Baum, L Frank, 97, 99, 101

beat generation, 27
beatchik, 28
beatnik, 1, 27–28
bebop, 26–27, 30–31, 34
Beethoven, 9, 105
Belloc, Hilaire, 104
Benedictines, 79, 107
Berlin, Irving, 162
Bhagavad Gita, 48
Bierce, Ambrose, 130
Black Elk, 158–163
Blake, William, 161
Book of Kells, 158
Borges, Jorge Luis, 130
Boudica, 84
Brooks, Phillips, 180
Brothers Grimm, 97
Brown, Oliver, 65
Budapest, 116
Buddhist, 38, 49, 63
Burroughs, William, 62
Byzantine, 118
Caesar, Sid, 29
Caesareum, 90–91
Cahokia, 162
Calloway, Cab, 30
Calypso, 98
Canton, 178, 180
Captain Video, 39
Cartesian, 168
Casimir the Great, 117
cerebral apartments, 8

Chang'an, 136
chaos theory, 169
Charlemagne, 5
Charles V, 123
chema, 59
Chief Joseph, 160, 162–163
Chinese jazz, 30
Chopin, Kate, 89–90
Cleopatra, 84
Colombia, 129–130
commune, 10
Congregationalism, 50
Constitution, 10, 23, 50
Cool School, 30
Copernicus, 57
Copland, 146
Corpus Hermeticum, 57
Cosmographiæ, 96
Crazy Horse, 158
Ctesiphon, 96
cynical constructivism, 29
da Vinci, Leonardo, 6, 55
Dalai Lama, 135
Danube, 105, 117–118
Danzig, 118
Dark Ages, 84
Davis, Miles, 30
de Crèvecoeur, Saint John, 178
Defoe, Daniel, 134
Delphian, 136
Depression, 13, 18, 124, 158
Der Rosenkavalier, 103
Desmond, Paul, 31
de Tocqueville, Alexis, 29
Dickens, Charles, 52
Disney, Walt, 15
dissociation, 109
Dixieland, 30–31
Dneiper, 117–118

Dniester, 118
Doctor Who, 39
Don, 118
doo-wop, 31–34
Dos Passos, John, 21
Douglass, Frederick, 65, 68 187
Downing, George, 10
Dr. Strangelove, 41
Druids, 135, 154
Dual Monarchy, 105, 116
DuBois, WEB, 67–68
Dylan, Bob, 161–164
educational television, 149, 153
Eisenhower, Dwight D, 12
Elbe, 118
Eliot, TS, 80–81
Emerson, Ralph Waldo, xi, 47, 80, 183, 187
Empress of China, 178
ESP, 61
ethics, xii, 3, 29, 70, 85, 87, 110, 126, 128, 149, 157
Eurocentrism, 9
Explorer, 17
Fallingwater, 146
Farnesworth, Philo T, 152
Faulkner, William, 21, 89, 133, 188
Fellini, Federico, 181
Ferguson, John H, 65
Ficino, Marsilio, 57–59
Foster, Stephen, 24
Foucault, Michel, 157
Frank, Waldo, 20
Franklin, Benjamin, xi, 100
French Impressionists, 8
Freud, Sigmund, 107
Fuentes, Carlos, 130
Fuller, Buckminster, 9

futurist, 9, 134
Gandhi, Mahatma, 157
Gershwin, George, 162
Getz, Stan, 31
Gibbon, Edward, 90
GI Bill, 11
Gilgamesh, 98
Gillespie, Dizzy, 26, 30, 186
Ginsberg, Allen, 28, 161
Giotto (di Bondone), 97
Giza, 4
Gnostics, 63
Goethe, Johann Wolfgang von, 7, 143, 184
Grande Ronde, 160
Great War, 14, 124
Gropius, Walter Adolph Georg, 144
Guthrie, Woody, 162
Hagia Sophia, 135
Hannibal, 181
Hapsburg, 104
Haydn, Franz Joseph, 105
Hellenism, 59, 84
Helsingør, 136
Hemingway, Ernest, 21, 82, 89, 187
Hermes Trismegistus, 59
Hindu, 48, 125, 131–132, 157
hippie trail, 131
Ho Chí Minh, 69
hobo, 20
hobohemians, 20
Hofburg, 105, 107–108
Hofmannsthal, Hugo von, 103
Holger the Dane, 136
Homer, 98–99
Hopi, 160
Huns, 66

Hussars, 117
hysteria, 85–87
Iceni, 84
Illimani, 127
immortality, 98–101, 137
In Dios, 182
Inca, 126
Indochina, 4, 70
Inquisition, 123
intended relevance, 181
Ithaca, 98
Iticaca, 126
Jainism, 49
James, Henry, 183
James, William, 181
Jara, Víctor, 130
Java, 4
Jefferson, Thomas, 38, 51–52, 100, 160
Jonson, Ben, 62
Juras, 116
Justinian, 135
Kafka, 62
Kaiser, 51
Kant, Immanuel, 75
karma, 48
Kaw, 101
Keats, John, 8
Kern, Jerome, 162
Kerouac, Jack, 11, 27, 186
Keynes, John Maynard, 15
Khan, 136
Klee, Paul, 144
Klimt, Gustav, 106
Kovacs, Ernie, 29
Kraków, 24, 118
Kronborg, 136
La Paz, 127
lacrosse, 166

laderas, 127
Lakota, 158–159, 163
Lao-Tsu, 38
law of natural rejection, 80
Le Corbusier, 144
Leaky, Louis, 66, 71
leisure problem, 11
Levittown, 11
Lewis and Clark, 163
Lewis, Sinclair, 21
Liebling, AJ, 63
Limoges, 5
Lincoln, Abraham, 69, 182
Llosa, Mario Vargas, 130
lost generation, 27
LSD, 62
Lukacs, John, 120
Machu Pichu, 135
Madison, James, 52
Magna Carta, 10
mahatma, 76–77
Malaysia, 4
Malcolm X, 69–70
Mandan, 163
Mandarin, xii, 124, 184–185
Manhattan Project, 14
Márquez, Gabriel García, 130
Marxist, 127
mass culture, 15
May, Elaine, 12–13
Maya, 24, 136
mazurka, 118
McLuhan, Marshall, 149, 153
Medici, 57
Mencken, HL, xi, 114, 119, 183
Merlin, 135
metaphor, 9, 16, 80, 103, 116, 133, 150–152, 161, 177
metaphysics, 26, 34, 51, 114, 185

metempsychosis, 49
metonymy, 151
Miles van der Rohe, Ludwig, 144–145
Ming Dynasty, 179
Minnesänger, 104
Monet, Claude, 97
Monk, Thelonius, 30, 122
Monticello, 51
More, Thomas, 96
Mozart, Wolfgang Amadeus, 8, 24
Munchkins, 25, 97
Musil, Robert, 103
Mycenaean, 115
Napoleon (Bonaparte), 51
NASA, 39
NATO, 70
Navajo, 158
negro, 67, 69
Neihardt, John, 159
Newton, Isaac, 168–169, 171, 173
Nez Perce, 160
Nibelung, 104
Nichols, Mike, 12
nihilistic phenomenology, 29
Nine Days in One Year, 42
nirvana, 147
Novalis, 23
Novum Organum, 58
Oder, 117–118
Odets, Clifford, 22
Odin, 99, 101
Odysseus, 98
Offenbach, Jacques, 100
Oglala Sioux, 159
O'Keeffe, Georgia, 25
Olduvai Gorge, 66
Oliver, King, 30

On the Beach, 41
O'Neill, Eugene, 22, 123, 188
Oz, 97, 99, 101
Paderewski, Ignacy Jan, 97
Pallavas, 4
Parable of Forty, 77–78
paranoid literature, 62
Paris, 5, 100, 101, 104
Parker, Charlie 'Bird', 30
Parkgasse, 102
passe-partout, 131
Peace Corps, 125–126, 131
Pearl River, 178
Penelope, 98–99
Pentateuch, 79
Pepper, Art, 31
Petra, 135
Philip of Spain, 123–124, 127
Piast Dynasty, 117
Picketwire, 95
Plato, 57, 59 83–84, 88, 98–99, 133, 134
Pleasure Dome, 136
Plessy, Homer, 65
Poe, Edgar Allen, xi, 8, 38, 134
Polanie, 117
Porter, Cole, 162
postmodern, 142–146
Potala, 135
Pound, Ezra, 21, 102, 188
Preseli Hills, 135
Professor Quatermass, 43
Prometheus, 4
psychic phenomena, 61
Ptolemaic, 58
public television, 152–153
Pueblo, 159
pure democracy, 49
Purgatoire, 95

quadrivium, 82
quantum theory, 38, 43, 168, 174
quarks, 63
Ragnar Hairy-Breeks, 5
rebop, 29–30
Republic, 10, 50, 98, 177, 180, 181, 183
Rheims, 5
Richard III, 75
Riesenrad, 105
Ringstrasse, 106, 108
Rogers, Will, 29
Roosevelt, Theodore, 75
Rumi, 147
Sabin, Albert, 56
Saint Catherine, 91
Saint Helena, 51
Saint Wenceslaus, 118
Saint-Cyr, 51
Salk, Jonas, 56
Samland, 115
Sandhurst, 51
Sanskrit, 48–49, 54, 76, 131
Sappho, 84
Sargent, John Singer, 24
sarsen, 135
satori, 49
Schönbrunn, 105
Schubert, 105
science fantasy, 37
science fiction, 37–42
Schiller, Johann Christoph Freiedrich von, 184
Scots, 7, 127, 189
Scott, Sir Walter, 68
Seagram Building, 145
Secession, 106, 124
Shakespeare, William, 75
Shoshone, 162–163

Shwedagon Pagoda, 135
Sims, Zoot, 31
Sinhalese, 131
Slovenes, 116
Socrates, 98
Sousa, John Philip, 100–101
Sputnik, 17, 41
Stadtpark, 105
Stara Zagora, 120
Stein, Gertrude, 21, 27, 187
Steinbeck, John, 22
Stevenson, Adlai, 12
Stitt, Sonny, 31
Strauss, Johann, 103, 105, 106
subculture, 27, 32, 61, 63
Sufi, 63, 147
Suleiman the Magnificent, 104
Summa Theologiæ, 54
Swift, Jonathan, 134
synecdoche, 151–152
Taliesin West, 146
Tantrics, 63
Taoist, 63
television obscenity, 155
tempo di valse, 102, 106
tempora quadragesima, 76
terra incognita, 132, 158
terra nostra, 132
Teutonic, 7, 67, 86, 118
Thoreau, Henry David, vii, 80
Thurber, James, 22
Tisza, 4, 118
Topeka Board, 65
Topkapi, 136
Toynbee, Arnold, 181
trilithons, 135
Trojan War, 98
Twain, Mark, xi, 18, 101, 113, 121, 186

UFO, 61
Urals, 115
Valkyrie, 95, 99–100
Vanderbilt, Cornelius, 101
Vanguard, 17
Vedic, 131
Verne, Jules, 37, 134
Vespucci, Amerigo, 96
Vienna, 91, 102–111, 115
Vietnam, 69–70
Vikings, 5, 24, 136, 182, 185
vindobona, 104
Viracocha, 126
Vistula, 117–118
vital nature, 58
Vizier Kara Mustafa, 104
Vogelweide, Walther von der, 104
Voltaire, 3
Vonnegut, Kurt, 62
Wagner, Otto, 106
Waldseemüller, Martin, 96
Washington, 12, 28, 108
wasichus, 159, 163
Wei Yuan, 179
Wells, HG, 134
Whigs, 127
Whirling Dervish, 147, 155
Whitman, Walt, 78–81, 161
Wittgenstein, Ludwig, 102, 110
Wolfe, Thomas, 21
Wright, Frank Lloyd, 144–146
Xanadu, 136
Yggdrasil, 76
Young, Lester, 30
Your Show of Shows, 29
Zen, 49, 63, 131, 159
Zuni, 160
Zwölf Apostelkeller, 109

www.ingramcontent.com/pod-product-compliance
Lightning Source LLC
Chambersburg PA
CBHW031953080426
42735CB00007B/378